Dedicated to the Holy Remnant who
earnestly contend for the faith.

I wish to express my sincere thanks to Travis & Amelia Crane for their labor in editing and revising this second edition.

*In Defense of
the Authenticity of*
1 John 5:7

Second Edition

C. H. Pappas ThM

Copyright © 2016 C. H. Pappas ThM.

All rights reserved. No part of this book may be used or reproduced by any means, graphic, electronic, or mechanical, including photocopying, recording, taping or by any information storage retrieval system without the written permission of the author except in the case of brief quotations embodied in critical articles and reviews.

Scripture taken from the King James Version of the Holy Bible.

WestBow Press books may be ordered through booksellers or by contacting:

WestBow Press
A Division of Thomas Nelson & Zondervan
1663 Liberty Drive
Bloomington, IN 47403
www.westbowpress.com
1 (866) 928-1240

Because of the dynamic nature of the Internet, any web addresses or links contained in this book may have changed since publication and may no longer be valid. The views expressed in this work are solely those of the author and do not necessarily reflect the views of the publisher, and the publisher hereby disclaims any responsibility for them.

Any people depicted in stock imagery provided by Thinkstock are models, and such images are being used for illustrative purposes only.
Certain stock imagery © Thinkstock.

ISBN: 978-1-4908-9247-4 (sc)
ISBN: 978-1-4908-9246-7 (e)

Library of Congress Control Number: 2015919167

Print information available on the last page.

WestBow Press rev. date: 02/15/2018

Contents

Preface	vii
Introduction	xix
1. The External Evidence	1
2. The Witness of the Church	20
3. Why the Comma in Few Greek Manuscripts	29
4. The Internal Witness	43
5. Further Discussion of the Internal Witness	55
6. Reflections	64
7. Exposing the Critics	78
8. The Revision Committees	95
Appeal to the Reader	99
Appendix	105
Bibliography	135

Preface

The writer recalls that there was a time when godly men with convictions would stand in their pulpits, affirming the infallibility of the Scriptures. The saints throughout the centuries also embraced this doctrine with unwavering conviction. The Scriptures were rightly revered as Holy Oracles, the Voice from Beyond, the Word of the Living God. Therefore, by virtue of the Scriptures being God's Word, it was understood that they, like Him, are infallible. But through the years, there has been a gradual falling away. Presently, there are few professing Christians who dare confess to the inerrancy of the Sacred Scriptures.

As a young man sitting in the pew, the writer, as many like himself, was not aware of what was taking place in the academic realm. Behind the scenes, ungodly men crept in unaware and gradually took over our citadels of learning. What they could not have taken by a frontal assault, they were able to capture through subtle infiltration. Once they infiltrated our schools, they began to sow their tares. When they were brought into question, they cried, "Academic freedom." It was not long thereafter that our schools were leavened with heresies. Such schools as Princeton, Harvard, and Yale, to mention a few, fell into the hands of the ungodly who had infiltrated their ranks.

Jan Karel Van Baalen, early in the twentieth century, addressed this calamity that plagues the church of the Living God. He wrote:

> Of later years Unitarian tactics have changed somewhat. Ministers with Unitarian convictions are now advised to stay in the orthodox churches, and work "from within." This procedure is called "strategic" by Dr. Slaten of the West Side Unitarian Church, New York; it is recommended by Dr. Palmer, the editor of the Harvard Theological Review; while Dr. J.W. Day, a leading Unitarian minister, writes, "A good many Unitarians are doing more good where they are than they could do anywhere else. They are undoubtedly capturing strongholds that we could never carry by direct attack. They are Modernists of Protestantism who are working from within the fold ... We want more of them and we want them where they are."[1]

The infiltration of ungodly men into the ranks of the saints is nothing new. Jude warned the saints of this very thing. In Jude 4, we read, "For there are certain men crept in unawares, who were before of old ordained to this condemnation, ungodly men, turning the grace of our God into lasciviousness, and denying the only Lord God, and our Lord Jesus Christ." Ungodly men infiltrated the Anglican

---

1 Jan Karel Van Baalen, *The Chaos of the Cults* (Grand Rapids, MI: WM. B. Eerdmans Publishing Co., 1958), 289.

In Defense of the Authenticity of 1 John 5:7

Church, and many sat on the Revision Committee. These men succeeded in mutilating the Authorized Version.

The above statement is quite strong. Can it be substantiated? It most certainly can. The Revision Committee in England was only to be composed of churchmen of the Anglican Church. No others were to undertake the editing of the Authorized Version of the Bible. However a Unitarian, Dr. Vance Smith, was received by the committee to sit with the revisionists while revising the Scriptures. Dr. Smith openly denied the deity of our Lord. Though many in England protested in outrage, Dr. Smith was never removed.[2] This was because the committee was filled with liberal theologians.[3] These were the kind of men of which Van Baalen wrote of in regard to heresies that plagued the church. But in this instance, the ungodly, instead of sowing seeds of heresy, went to the extreme; they mutilated the Holy Scriptures.

The American Standard Committee was organized in 1871 upon the invitation of the Revision Committee in England. By October 1872, the Revision Committee in America was in full swing. Now both committees were actively working together to revise the Scriptures. However, the American Revision Committee was made up of scholars selected from different denominations. Thus the English Revision Committee, in working together with the Revision Committee in the United States, was made up of less than half of the churchmen of the Anglican Church.[4] Dr. Joseph Henry Thayer was a consultant on the Revision Committee while serving in the States and labored with the committee on the American Standard Version. He too was a Unitarian

---

2   David O. Fuller, *Which Bible* 2nd Ed. (Grand Rapids, MI: Grand Rapids International Publications, 1972), 291.
3   (Fuller, Which Bible 296-297)
4   (Fuller, Which Bible 288-289)

who openly denied the deity of our Lord. This is not to mention Dr. Philip Schaff, who headed the American Standard Committee. He sought to Romanize the church in America.[5]

The reader should also be aware that Dr. Schaff held to a very poor view of the inspiration of the Scriptures. For example, Dr. Schaff made a horrible contrast between the writings of Paul and James on the matter of justification. He writes, "The Epistle of James stands at the head of the Catholic Epistles, so called, and represents the first and lowest stage of Christian knowledge."[6]

Later in a footnote he wrote:

> So also Renan and Weiffenbach (Liberals) assert without proof that James organized a Jewish counter-mission to undermine Paul. But in this case, James, as a sensible and practical man, ought to have written to the Gentile Christians, and not to the "twelve tribes," who needed no warning against Paul and his doctrine. His epistle (that is James Epistle) represents simply an earlier and lower form of Christianity ignorant of the higher, yet preparatory to it, as the preaching of John the Baptist prepared the way for that of Christ. It was written without any reference to Paul, probably before the Council of Jerusalem and before the circumcision controversy, in the earliest stage of the apostolic church as it described in the

---

5 David O. Fuller, *True or False* 2nd Ed. (Grand Rapids, MI: Grand Rapids International Publications, 1983), 289.

6 Philip Schaff, *History of the Christian Church* (Grand Rapids, MI: WM. B. Eerdmans Publishing Co., 1985), Vol. 1, 520.

In Defense of the Authenticity of 1 John 5:7

first chapter of Acts, when Christianity was not yet clearly distinguished and finally separated from the Jews.[7]

To Dr. Schaff, the Bible was still a seven-sealed book. He had no idea what it said. If he had eyes to see, he would discover that there were no contradictions between James and Paul. James, as Paul, was a mere penman of Scriptures. The Author of the Scriptures is the Holy Spirit, and there is no contradiction in Him. The biblical man always understood the Scriptures to be the voice of God regardless of whom the penman might have been. For example, in Acts 1:16 we read, "Men and brethren, this Scripture must needs have been fulfilled, which the Holy Ghost by the mouth of David spake before concerning Judas, which was guide to them that took Jesus."

The reader should observe in the above text that the Holy Ghost spoke by the mouth of David. David was the instrument through which God spoke, not the author! God is the one who speaks. Hence it is not the men but the Scriptures that are inspired. Holy men of God no doubt were borne along by the Spirit; but it is God who speaks (2 Pet. 2:21). If men do not realize this fundamental truth concerning the Word of God, then they have no business handling the Sacred Oracles!

The only reason this is mentioned is to reveal to the reader something of the character of the men who revised the Holy Scriptures. More will be said of them later. However, it should be realized from the onset that these ungodly men had a tremendous influence on producing these new revisions of the Scriptures. This is apparent by what was said; these men did not believe that God is the Author of the written Word. Therefore, they handled the Scriptures as

---

7   (Schaff, History of the Christian Church, Vol. 1 520-521)

a piece of profane literature. Is it any wonder that these men would carelessly remove the Comma from the Sacred Text!

The Scriptures are indeed the infallible Word of God. At one time, the doctrine of the inspiration, preservation, and infallibility of the Scriptures was never challenged. That is with the exception of those who were outside of the pales of the mainline church. These men were infidels and liberals, which are euphemisms for heretics. The church had always been plagued by such men. But there was a clear line of demarcation drawn between the two camps. However, those distinctions were set aside when these two committees came together to revise the Authorized Version. It seems that scholarship had become the common denominator, making all men acceptable!

For centuries there had been but one prominent English translation of the Scriptures, the Authorized Version. But with the emerging of the Revised Version of 1881, there was an open and brazen challenge of the doctrines of the inerrancy of the Word of God. Shortly thereafter, we were introduced to another Critical Bible, the American Standard Version of 1903. This version could have come out much earlier, it was withheld because of an agreement that they made that Revised Version would first be published. However, no credible pastor ever embraced either of those two translations. They tenaciously held to the Authorized Version. As late as 1970, it was not uncommon to hear pastors in large churches hold up the Authorized Version and passionately cry out to their congregations, "Do not let anyone take this Bible from you!"[8] This war cry coming from the pulpits indicated that the battle for the Bible had become critical.

---

8   Dr. Homer Lindsey Sr. of First Baptist Church, Jacksonville, Florida, was known to encourage his congregation in this way.

In Defense of the Authenticity of 1 John 5:7

Presently the climate has drastically changed. The curtains are fast falling upon the older generation. They will soon be removed from the stage. Another generation will come to take their place. But they are not prepared to take up the baton and carry it to the next generation. Instead of affirming the infallibility of the Scriptures, we hear men speak of the sufficiency of the Scripture. This is true—the Scriptures are indeed sufficient—but there is a world of difference between the sufficiency and the infallibility of the Scriptures. These are good men who for the most part have renounced the Authorized Version. As yet, they have not conceded on the doctrine of the authority of the Sacred Oracles. However, they have made some very serious concessions that will leave the coming generation, if our Lord tarries, with no place to stand.

In some respects, it may be understood why there has been such a drastic departure from the doctrine of the infallibility of the Scriptures. Professors in seminaries, Bible colleges, and Bible schools have labored to discredit the Scriptures and especially the Authorized Version. By intimidating their young scholars, alleging the Bible is filled with errors and discrepancies, they were in time able to wrest the Scriptures from them. These young scholars who entered into these schools were not equipped to meet these sophistries. Though some resisted for a season, they were finally won over by the wiles of their professors.

For an example, many of these students studied Greek while in seminary. They were given the Critical Greek Text. They knew nothing of its origin; nor were they told that there was another Greek text known as the *Textus Receptus*. That is, the Greek Bible that the church from its inception held. Hence, as they began to learn Greek, it was not long before they discovered that their Greek text was not in agreement with the Authorized Version. So rather than throwing off their Greek New Testament, they threw off the Authorized Version. Is it any wonder that now we have pastors who embrace one of the modern translations of the Scriptures such as the New American Standard Version or the New International Version?

Many preachers have not as yet given up the Sacred Scriptures but have conceded on the doctrine of the infallibility of the Scriptures. Their position is that the Bible contains the Word of God rather than that the Bible is the Word of God. This is evident in that both pulpit and pew alike have embraced either the New American Standard Version or the New International Version of the Bible. There are others who hold to some other translation from the Critical Greek Text, but the former two are the most popular. The originators of the Critical Greek Text, from which these new translations are taken, confessed that they did not produce an inerrant Bible.[9]

This is also apparent, as the Critical Text is constantly open to revisions and amending. This is not to mention many passages that are placed in brackets, bringing them into question. How can such a revision of the Scriptures be said to be the inerrant Word of God when multitudes of passages are brought into question by placing them in brackets? Therefore, these pastors, who embrace these new translations of the Bible, have unknowingly embarked upon a slippery slope that will eventually lead to the ruin of the church.

Today, no church of any size embraces the Authorized Version. This is very sad when we consider that the Authorized Version for four hundred years was the only Bible that believers in the English-speaking world embraced.

---

9 Brooke F. Westcott and Fenton J. A. Hort, *Introduction to the New Testament in the Original Greek* (Peabody, M.A: Hendrickson Publishers, 1998), Vol. 3, 271-272.

In Defense of the Authenticity of 1 John 5:7

Presently, if a church happens to embrace the Authorized Version, those saints are looked upon as a cult. The writer is forced to confess that there may be a few churches that might fall under that description, but these are very few. One does not take leave of one's senses to embrace the King James Version. Neither does one shut one's eyes to the facts. Men with sound minds, clear heads, and strong convictions hold and defend the Authorized Version. Better still, such men in an open debate will silence their critics.

Among the so-called new conservatives, the New American Standard has replaced the Authorized Version. These men unknowingly are a contradiction to themselves. Many of them, when asked, confess without any reservations that the Scriptures are inerrant. At the same time, they embrace a Bible that has multitudes of passages in brackets questioning their legitimacy. One passage has been brazenly omitted, with a footnote reading that some unknown pious scribe added the passage to the Scriptures. This passage, of course, is 1 John 5:7. This is not to mention the various readings that have been altered. With the questioning of many passages, the altering of readings, and now the removal of an entire passage from the Scriptures, how can one in all honesty confess unconditional trust in these new Bibles?

One of the things the writer has discovered over the years is that those who attack the Authorized Version are either dishonest or deceived. Most of these men are deceived, and it is with meekness that they should be addressed. We are commanded, "In meekness instructing those that oppose themselves; if God peradventure will give them repentance to the acknowledging of the truth" (2 Tim. 2:25). Our mission is not to condemn but to lead men to repentance.

However, what the writer has also discovered over the years is that those who oppose the Authorized Version, when forced to yield in one area, change horses and attack from another direction. For example, when the scientific methods of the Critical School of Textual Criticism are shown to be utter nonsense, these critics do not repent but rather change course. Some of these men have put together what is presently referred to as the Majority Text. What is arresting is there are two different Majority Texts on the market. No doubt, in the future there will be a third and a fourth and on and on. The number will climb as new manuscripts are discovered. Thus, the same objective is still attained—the denial of the infallibility and preservation of the Scriptures. Men are still searching for the Word of God, which God had promised to preserve to all generations (Ps. 12:6-7; Matt. 24:35). The issue is not so much the preference of one translation over another but rather, the casting of doubt upon the inerrancy of the Scriptures.

One can readily see how the enemy, Satan, unceasingly attacks God's Word. Satan has not changed. He assaulted the progenitors of our race by asking, "…hath God said…" (Gen. 3:1). The old serpent is still asking the same question and will continue to do so until our Lord returns. His desire is to cast suspicion upon the Sacred Oracles. If this is accomplished, he then will openly deny the Word of God. He continues to work in and through deceived men and is determined to take the Word of God out of the hands and hearts of the people in order to damn their souls.

Even though this work focuses mainly upon a singular passage of the Scriptures, it addresses a much larger issue, the inerrancy and preservation of the Scriptures. If 1 John 5:7, known as the Comma or the Johanneum Comma, can be discredited and removed from the Scriptures, as it has been in the new translations of the Scriptures, then who is to say that any of the other passages of the Scriptures that are presently questioned will not at some later date also be removed?

Our Lord has clearly promised, "…Till heaven and earth pass, one jot or one tittle shall in no wise pass from the law…" (Matt. 5:18). And again in Matthew 24:35, "Heaven and earth shall pass away, but my words shall not pass away." Observe "words" is in the plural. Not one word of Holy Scriptures shall be lost. How much more then shall He preserve an entire passage of the Scriptures men are bent in removing from the Sacred Text!

> My faith has found a resting place,
> Not in device nor creed;
> I trust the Ever living One,
> His wounds for me shall plead.
>
> My Heart is leaning on the Word,
> The written Word of God
> Salvation by my Saviour's Name,
> Salvation thro' His blood.
>
> I need no other argument,
> I need no other plea,
> It is enough that Jesus died,
> and that He died for me.[10]

---

10 Lidie H. Edmunds, *Favorite Hymns of the Faith* (Wheaton, IL: Tabernacle Publishing Co., 1974), 193.

Introduction

In August of 1992, the writer was invited to attend a meeting in Jacksonville, Florida, held by Reformed Presbyterians. Dr. A. M., a professor from Reformed Theological Seminary in Orlando, Florida, led the meeting. He presented a paper on "The Family of God." It was an excellent paper that showed true scholarship. Later when we were taking a break, Dr. M. noticed my Bible; it was the King James Version. It immediately drew his attention, as well as those who were in the room, for they all held to either the New International Version or the New American Standard Version. No one other than the writer in that gathering of conservative scholars held to the Authorized Version.

Dr. M., in his amazement, asked, "Do you still use the King James Version?" When he asked the question, it was not with contempt. He was actually astonished. It seemed incredible to him that anyone in this day of such enlightenment would still be holding to the Authorized Version. This was quite difficult for him to accept. However, I, too, was startled by his question. It was equally as hard for me to accept that a scholar of his capacity should hold to a copy of the Critical Text like the NAS or the NIV. To his question came the unequivocal reply, "Yes, sir, I do."

Then the doctor immediately broke out in laughter. He was not being scornful, but rather he was startled. My answer took him by surprise. It was as if what he had heard was incredible. He then immediately inquired, "Do you accept 1John 5:7?" He challenged that particular passage because it is the least-attested-to passage in the Greek manuscripts. It has been removed from new translations of the New Testament. It was not surprising that the attack upon the Authorized Version always, without failure, commences by questioning this text. Again, my response was, "Yes, sir, I most certainly do."

The doctor again laughed in unbelief. It was inconceivable to him that anyone in this day and age would still hold to that passage. They had removed it from all the new translations of the Scriptures. As far as he was concerned, it had been tried in the courts, and it was found lacking. Then he said, "Why, no one believes that anymore! It is not found in any of the early manuscripts."

"That may be true," I responded, "but you will find 1 John 5:7 quoted by Cyprian, who predates the earliest manuscripts by one hundred years, if not more." With that, there came a blank stare upon his face. The smile on his face immediately vanished. What flooded into his mind at that moment? One can only assume. It might have been that he could not believe anyone would dare argue in defense of this passage. In the past, there have been many fiery debates over the Comma, but the flames that once raged are now extinguished. Would one dare seek to revive those old debates out of those ashes! Or it might have been that light broke upon his mind and he was stunned. But the former most likely was true since the conversation came to an abrupt end. With that, he turned and walked away. No

In Defense of the Authenticity of 1 John 5:7

more was to be said; the issue, as far as he was concerned, was closed. As for the Comma, his position was not open to debate. He adopted the position of the School of Higher Textual Criticism. He, with Dr. Scrivener, concluded that the Comma was a deformity in our English Bible.[11]

Since then, the writer has discovered that there were renewed attacks upon the Authorized Version. These were coming from the so-called Majority Text Advocates. It is amazing how these men who, for the most part, reject the Critical Text were, at the same time, presenting some of the same arguments. As different as they might be on some issues, they agree upon one thing; they both reject the Comma. The writer at the time was not aware that this deception was as great as it was. He was not aware that these renewed attacks were coming from the supposed ranks of grassroots conservative evangelicals. In the past, such attacks came only from the ranks of the infidels, liberals, modernists, and Unitarians. But now, they are coming from those who are looked upon as the guardians of the faith.

First John 5:7 is not the only passage these men questioned. However, this passage is looked upon as being the least credible of all the passages that are presently questioned. The other passages in question are still placed in brackets. But as for the Comma, it has been entirely removed from the Bible. At one time, it too was in brackets, like many of the other passages, but not anymore. Therefore, when people attack the integrity of the Authorized Version, 1 John 5:7 is inevitably challenged. They argue that it is an aberration that has entered into the Holy Text through some pious scribe. The court had made its ruling, and it is not about to rescind its verdict. What is even worse, as far as they are concerned, the case is sealed and not to be reopened. It is the

---

[11] Frederick H. A. Scrivener, *Six Lectures on the Text of the New Testament* (London, England: George Bell and Sons, 1875), 58.

contention of the writer that the arguments for the Comma need to be again resounded in the ears of this generation. The arguments on behalf of the Comma that have been silenced by the present critics need to be brought to light. This little book is written in the defense of the Johanneum Comma with hope that light might break forth upon the minds of the people of God who strive to cling to the truth. The writer's prayers are that the past rulings on the Comma might be overturned. But if that is not accomplished, then by all means his prayers are for the faithful remnant; may they be encouraged to steadfastly contend for the faith. There is still a remnant who cleaves to the truth. There are still a people who cling to the Authorized Version. There are still faithful people who have not been swept away by the wiles of the evil one. This is by the grace of Our Living God and Savior, our Lord Jesus Christ.

Though this little book is a theological work, it is written so that the blue-collar worker seeking the truth may read it and walk away comprehending what is said. It is not written for the scholar but rather for the people who sit in the pews. Nevertheless, the scholar, in reading this polemic, will also be challenged by what is said, for there is much said to provoke thought. As for those who reject the Comma, it is the writer's prayer that they may reconsider their position in the light of the evidence that is set forth. No man who is honest with the evidence set forth can with good conscience reject the Trinitarian passage.

Arguments will be brought from both external and internal evidences as well as answering the question of why so few Greek manuscripts testify to the Comma. The work will also address some questions that will provoke thought even from those who strongly reject the Johanneum Comma. In conclusion, the writer will address the crux of the problem and expose the fallacy of the modern textual critics. Thus, this book will enable the reader to understand the essence of the problem with which we are faced.

> Holy Bible, Book divine,
> Precious treasure, thou art mine:
> Mine to tell me whence I came,
> Mine to teach me what I am.
>
> Mine to chide me when I rove,
> Mine to show a Saviour's love,
> Mine thou art to guide and guard,
> Mine to punish or reward,
>
> Mine to comfort in distress-
> Suffering in this wilderness,
> Mine to show-by living faith-
> Man can triumph over death.
>
> Mine to tell of joys to come,
> And the rebel sinner's doom:
> O Thou holy Book divine,
> Precious treasure, thou art mine![12]

---

[12] John Burton, *Favorite Hymns of the Faith* (Wheaton, IL: Tabernacle Publishing Co. 1974), 253.

Chapter 1

The External Evidence

The external evidences that will be presented in this chapter are those witnesses apart from the text itself that testify to the authenticity of the Comma. These witnesses are far stronger than many are aware. They are also far more plentiful, as these witnesses are not a few. Neither are these witnesses to be slighted, as many attempt to do. But rather, they must be heard, for they are viable witnesses testifying to the validity of the Trinitarian passage. In many respects, it may surprise the reader to discover just how strongly they attest to the Comma, which was first marked off in brackets and presently removed from the new translations of the Scriptures. In this chapter, these witnesses will be presented one by one, and in turn, the reader will be left to make up his or her mind after he or she weighs the evidences that are presented.

The first witnesses that must not be ignored are the Greek manuscripts themselves. This may sound strange, as the Greek manuscripts are often cited as a witness against the Comma. However, at the same time, the Greek manuscripts indisputably bear witness to the Comma. We are told that there are only nine Greek manuscripts that bear witness to the Trinitarian passage. However George Travis in rebuking Gibbon's pointed out that Stephen catalogued 31 Greek manuscripts that bore witness to the disputed passage, (Letters to Edward George Gibbon, Esq. *Forgotten Books* p. 285) Hence there are far more Greek Manuscripts that bear witness to 1 John 5:7 than what we are told. Nevertheless, for arguments sake, we will argue from the nine witnesses which the modern critics acknowledge. But the reader must never think that there are only nine Greek Manuscripts that contain the disputed passage. However the facts cannot be skirted when we consider that there are indisputably nine Greek manuscripts that bear witness to the Comma.

These manuscripts are catalogued for us: 61, 88, 221, 429, 629, 635, 636, 918, and 2381. Dr. Scrivener mentions 162, which is the same as 629. Of this manuscript, Dr. Scrivener says, "There is little suspicion cast."[13] In other words, this manuscript is to be accepted.

Some seek to denigrate their witness, claiming that of these nine Greek manuscripts, four of them have the disputed passage in the margin, and five of them have it in the text itself. These manuscripts are said to be of late date and therefore are given very little weight. The earliest manuscript that contains the Comma is from the tenth century, manuscript 221 as introduced above, and then the passage is in the margin. Thus contemporary critics assume that the Comma is an interpolation. At best, they affirm that the witness for the Comma is extremely weak in the light of 5,500 Greek manuscripts, with only nine testifying on its behalf.

However, the above numbers are overinflated. We only have in our possession about five hundred Greek manuscripts of the epistle of 1 John. Furthermore, some

---

13 (Scrivener, Six Lectures on the Text of the New Testament 203)

of these manuscripts are but mere fragments. Also, some of these manuscripts do not even have this portion of Scripture in question. So the numbers they throw out are exaggerated to the extreme. These men are either not honest or they are ignorant. I leave the judging to the reader. Nevertheless, it is true that the majority of the extant Greek manuscripts of the epistle of 1 John do not contain the Comma. But these numbers must not be exaggerated.

Another charge brought against the mentioned manuscripts is that they are of a late date and thus their testimony is not credible. In addressing this problem, it also should be understood that the dating of manuscripts is foolish as well as meaningless. We should never be carried away with such sophistries. If the reader stops for a moment and considers, he or she will realize that one copy is just as authentic as any other copy, if it is a legitimate copy of the Original Autograph. Just because the copy is of a late date does not make it less credible. A copy is a copy, regardless of the date. It is important that the reader becomes aware of this fundamental truth. If one fails to grasp this central truth, then one may be led astray by the false assumption that the earlier copies of the Scriptures are more reliable. To hold to such a position is to deny the doctrine of the preservation of the Scriptures, which our Lord clearly taught (Matt. 24:35).

Nevertheless, there are those who insist that the older the manuscript, the more genuine it is. In light of this deception, it would interest the reader to discover what Dr. Scrivener had to say about the ancient manuscripts and especially of the two oldest manuscripts we presently possess. He wrote:

> And here it may be observed once and for all, that every known manuscript of high antiquity is thus altered by later scribes, usually for the

> purpose of amending manifested faults, or of conforming the reading to the one in vogue at a more recent date. Codex B (Vaticanus) we trace two or three such revisers; in Codex Aleph (Sinaiticus) at least 10, some of whom spread their work systematically over every page ...[14]

What an incriminating statement this is upon all the older manuscripts! All of the oldest manuscripts were altered and amended—not merely some of them or most of them but all of them! And the reason for these alterations and amendments was because of their corruption! This is the testimony of one of the most credible textual critics who sat on the Revision Committee.

As for the Vaticanus and the Sinaiticus that are revered by contemporary critics, these are without question among the most corrupt manuscripts in our possession. The critics of the School of Lower Textual Criticism did not revere the older manuscripts as contemporary critics do. Yet these two corrupt manuscripts are cited against the Comma! It is said that the Comma is not found in any of these older manuscripts. However, those manuscripts are corrupt! They must not be cited as evidence against the Trinitarian passage.

It is apparent that the great Erasmus did not value the Vaticanus. When he was laboring on his edition of the Greek New Testament, he had access to the Vaticanus. Even though the Vatican jealously guarded this manuscript because of its antiquity, Erasmus nevertheless had access to it. Dr. Scrivener rightly points out, "The Papal Librarian Paul Bombasius sent some accounts of it to the great Erasmus in 1521."[15] However, Erasmus did not trouble himself with it as contemporary critics do. He found the later–dated

---

14 (Scrivener, Six Lectures on the Text of the New Testament 48)
15 (Scrivener, Six Lectures on the Text of the New Testament 29)

Greek manuscripts far more weighty and acceptable than the earlier-dated manuscripts. He ignored the Vaticanus altogether. The only explanation for the survival of these old manuscripts, which the contemporary critics idolize, is because of their corruption. The church never used them. If they had, then they would have been worn out and burned. So banish the thought that the oldest manuscripts are the best. The truth of the matter is, the older the manuscripts, the worse they are. The best manuscripts we possess are of a later date. More shall be said on this subject.

It may be surprising to some that we do not possess the Original Autograph. But we have many copies of the Original Autograph. It is important that this is understood. God preserved His Word by faithfully guiding the transmission of the Scriptures to all generations (Ps. 12:6–7; Ps. 100:5). With this understood, we need to examine some of the confessions of conservative Christians. They read, "I believe in the inerrancy of the Holy Scriptures in the Original Autograph." (Southern Baptist Confession of Faith and Practice) How does this confession apply to the Bible in our hands? We do not have the Original Autograph, which implies we do not have the pure Word of God. How, then, are we any different from the infidels who deny inerrancy?

The facts remain that we have copies of the Original Autograph. God has faithfully preserved His Word to all generations (Ps. 12:6–7; Matt. 24:35). No thanks to man, God has and is still doing just as He promised. He has well preserved His Word as we have in our possession multitudes of copies of the Original Autograph. Therefore, these confessions should be amended to read, "I believe in the inerrancy of the Holy Scriptures," period!

The Bible in our hands is the preserved Word of the Living God. It is without error. How is it that we have strayed from this position to confessions that are of no weight? It is because we have been influenced by the dating of manuscripts. This is an invention of those who deny the preservation and inspiration of the Scriptures. Modern critics are of the opinion that the Original Autograph can only be rediscovered as any other piece of ancient literature. They do not realize the obvious; we possess copies of the Original Autograph!

As for the Johanneum Comma, God has preserved it in spite of the deceitfulness of infamous men. It is found without question in nine Greek manuscripts. It may not be as pronounced as we would like it, but it is undeniably there. Although this may be said to be a weak witness, it is an indisputable witness. Whatever men may say, there is still the testimony of the Comma in the Greek manuscripts. There is an undeniable witness on behalf of the Trinitarian text. As much as many contemporary scholars do not like to acknowledge this fact, at the same time, neither can they deny it. The Comma is clearly preserved in nine of the Greek manuscripts! This is concrete fact and not a hypothetical assumption.

On the other hand, there are other witnesses who strongly attest to the Comma. One powerful witness testifying to the validity of the Comma is the Old Latin manuscripts. Sometimes these manuscripts are referred to as the Old Italic manuscripts. The evidence for the Comma becomes even more pronounced when we consider these Old Latin manuscripts of 1 John that we have in our possession. Although these manuscripts date from the sixth or seventh century to the thirteenth century, they are copies of earlier dated manuscripts that go as far back as the second and fourth centuries. Startling is the testimony of these Old Latin manuscripts. They all unanimously testify in favor of the disputed passage.

By some strange notion, it is believed that the Scriptures can only be preserved in the Greek manuscripts. Although

In Defense of the Authenticity of 1 John 5:7

the Greek manuscripts are the weightier witnesses, we must be careful not to ignore the testimony of the Old Latin manuscripts. For when the Scriptures were written in Greek, they were very soon thereafter translated into Latin. The Scriptures were quickly translated into Latin because Latin, as Greek at that time, was a universal language. Arthur W. Wainwright, in his book, *A Guide to the New Testament,* wrote, "Since there were two universal languages, Greek and Latin, a traveler could make himself understood in most parts of the world."[16] Therefore, it is no wonder that the Scriptures were quickly translated into Latin, which makes them a very powerful witness.

Scholars also unanimously agree that the Old Latin New Testament was translated from the Greek text about the second half of the second century.[17] This would be around AD 150. However, it is only fair to mention that other scholars date the Old Latin New Testament even earlier. These men date the Old Latin to have been translated from the Greek in or about AD 137. Hence, the Scriptures were translated into Latin about the same time or very shortly after the Greek New Testament Scriptures were completed. This claim is not disputed by any scholars of whom the writer is aware.

Therefore, in light of these facts, we must not look upon the Old Latin with contempt. The Old Latin manuscripts strongly testify in favor of the Comma. Their witness is exceedingly strong on behalf of the passage in question. Even though we possess but a few of these Old Latin manuscripts of 1 John, and even though they may not be

---

16 Arthur W. Wainwright, *A Guide to the New Testament* (London: Epworth Press, 1965), 15.
17 Frederick H. A. Scrivener, *A Plain Introduction to the New Testament Textual Criticism,* Vol.2, 4th Ed. (New York: George Bell & Sons, 1894), 43.

very good copies at that, they unanimously testify to the authenticity of the Trinitarian passage. This in itself is a very powerful testimony in favor of the authenticity of the disputed passage.

As for these Old Latin manuscripts of 1 John, we only possess six copies, and all six of them contain the Comma that has of late been brought into question. The Comma might not be worded exactly as we would like it, but these manuscripts indisputably testify to it. The list of these manuscripts for those that like cataloging manuscripts are as follows: *Monacensis 64, Speculum, Colbertinus, Demidovianus, Divionesis,* and *Perpinanensis.* The *Speculum* is a treatise or a collection of Bible passages that has the disputed passage. We may not want to refer to the *Speculum* as a copy of the Scriptures, but it should be acknowledged that the Comma is quoted twice in this one manuscript, which appears to be the oldest of these Old Latin manuscripts.

Another viable witness to the Comma is the Latin Vulgate. Of the Latin Vulgate, Scrivener states that perhaps, "49 out of 50 manuscripts testify to this disputed Comma."[18] This in itself is a very powerful testimony on behalf of the Trinitarian passage. One reason this is a very powerful witness on behalf of the disputed text is because Jerome omitted the Comma in his translation from the Old Latin into the Latin Vulgate! This may be the reason why Dr. Scrivener said that the Comma is not found in fifty of the best Latin Vulgate copies.[19] But again, we must not overlook the fact that there are over eight thousand Latin Vulgate manuscripts and 98 percent, if not more, testify on behalf of the disputed passage. Some estimate the extant manuscripts

---

18 (Scrivener, A Plain introduction to the New Testament Textual Criticism 403)
19 (Scrivener, Six Lectures on the Text of the New Testament 205)

of the Latin Vulgate to exceed ten thousand. Therefore, the Latin Vulgate is an exceedingly powerful witness on behalf of the Three Heavenly Witnesses. The question that we are confronted with is how did the Comma enter into the Latin Vulgate when Jerome omitted it?

The Trinitarian passage finally entered into the Latin Vulgate through its predecessor, the Old Latin. The Latin speaking world at that time was not ready to part with the Johanneum Comma. Thus, when the Vulgate was presented to the Latin–speaking world, there was a great outcry against Jerome and his new revision of the Latin Vulgate. Jerome's Vulgate departed in many respects from the Old Latin Bible, including the omission of the Comma. This caused a great disturbance in the churches throughout Europe and North Africa because they held adamantly to their Old Latin Bible. The people were so outraged that Jerome's Vulgate was never accepted. *Never!*

Helvidius, the great Waldensian scholar of northern Italy, accused Jerome of using corrupt manuscripts in producing the Vulgate.[20] Jovinian, another great scholar of northern Italy, also charged Jerome with the same crime. Their charges were just. A later study of Jerome's Vulgate was published by Sabatier and Bianchini. These scholars proved the point. They wrote, "It was obvious that though there were many points of difference, there were still traces of a common source."[21] All heretical manuscripts trace back to a common source. It was these many points of differences they mentioned that made Jerome's Vulgate unacceptable.

Therefore, it is understandable why the Latin–speaking world rejected Jerome's Vulgate. They would have no part of

---

20 Benjamin G. Wilkinson, *Our Authorized Bible* (Payson, AZ: Leaves-Of-Autumn Books, 1930), 33.

21 (Scrivener, A Plain Introduction to the New Testament Textual Criticism 42)

it. Only through much persecution, and a full nine hundred years later, was Jerome's Vulgate finally received.[22] Even then, it had to pass through many revisions. First John 5:7 was again reinserted. That is why forty–nine out of fifty Vulgate manuscripts testify to the Comma, which Jerome omitted. It is therefore apparent that the Comma was widely accepted and attested to in the Latin–speaking world before AD 384–385. This, among other things, reveals that there was a longstanding witness for the Comma that precedes the oldest Greek manuscript in our possession that is dated around AD 325.

Hence the witness for the Comma is far, far stronger than the Majority Text and the Critical Text advocates are willing to admit. It appears that they have placed all of their confidence upon the sole witness of the majority readings of Greek manuscripts or upon a few critical manuscripts of their choosing. Presently, many reject the Comma because it is not found in the two oldest manuscripts, the Sinaiticus and the Vaticanus. To lean upon these two manuscripts is to lean upon a reed that will pierce the hand.

It is said that if the Trinitarian passage was present in AD 325, Athanasius would most certainly have quoted it in his polemic on the deity of Christ. But this is an argument from silence. Furthermore, if one would read his polemic, one would discover that there were many other passages Athanasius omitted that testified to the deity of our Lord. What these men fail to acknowledge is that the Comma was in Athanasius' Bible. Athanasius, at the time of the first Ante- Nicene Council, was a deacon in the church of Alexandria. Therefore, it is safer to assume that he chose not to quote the passage than to assume that it was not in his copy of the Scriptures. If it were in Cyprian's copy of the

---

22 (Wilkinson 28)

In Defense of the Authenticity of 1 John 5:7

Scriptures more than a half of a century earlier, then it was most certainly in Athanasius' copy of the Scriptures. It goes without question that Athanasius had a copy of the Old Latin that was in use at the time.

Also keep in mind that it was sixty years later when Jerome produced the Latin Vulgate omitting the Comma. This in turn caused a great disturbance throughout the Latin–speaking world. All of this indicates that the Comma was well accepted at the time of the Ante–Nicene Council. Therefore, the Comma had to be in Athanasius' copy of the Scriptures. The argument presented that the Comma was not present in AD 325 or Athanasius would have quoted it falls short in light of the historical facts. However, Athanasius did allude to it in his polemic.

Many of the contemporary textual critics greatly labor to downplay the Latin Witness. What the reader should be aware of is that was not the position of Dr. W. F. Moulton, a prominent bishop who labored on the Revision Committee. If it were left up to him, he would have set aside the Greek manuscripts and produced the Revised Version based wholly upon the Latin manuscripts. He was one of the several liberals on the Revision Committee who was in opposition to the Byzantine manuscripts. He is quoted as saying, "The Latin translation, being derived from manuscripts more ancient than any we now possess, is frequently a witness of the highest value in regard to the Greek text which is current in the earliest times…its testimony is in many cases confirmed by Greek manuscripts which have been discovered or examined since the sixteenth century."[23]

The Old Latin and the Latin Vulgate are not the only external witnesses we have that testify on behalf of the Comma. But if these were the only witnesses we had,

---

23 (Fuller, Which Bible 288)

they would be sufficient, for they historically prove that the Comma was universally accepted by the churches centuries before the oldest manuscripts came into existence. Nevertheless, other witnesses will be cited.

We have strong witnesses coming forth from different versions, lexicons, and quotes of the early church fathers. But to these witnesses, the modern critics give very little credence. All these witnesses are subordinate to the Greek manuscripts. There is some merit to this position, but when it comes to such preponderance of evidences as those mentioned–the church fathers, the Old Latin, the Vulgate, and other translations of the Scriptures–surely there must be some consideration given to them. This is not to mention nine Greek manuscripts that also testify to its authenticity.

As for the church fathers, there is one the modern critics cannot ignore. This is Cyprian. Cyprian lived in the middle of the third century. He lived a hundred years before the earliest extant manuscript we have in our possession. Cyprian quotes 1 John 5:7 in his first treatise on the unity of the church. This was a universal letter written to the churches. All of this implies that the Comma was well accepted throughout Christendom. He wrote, "The Lord says, 'I and the Father are one;' and again it is written; 'the Father, and of the Son, and of the Holy Spirit,' [sic] 'and these three are one.'"[24] Scrivener wrote, "It is surely safe and more candid to admit that Cyprian read verse 7 in his copies than to resort to the explanation of Facundus (vi) that the holy bishop was merely putting on verse 8 a spiritual meaning."[25]

Even though Scrivener acknowledges that Cyprian read the passage in his copy of the Holy Scriptures, he

---

24 Cyprian, *The Ante-Nicene Fathers,* Translated by Rev. Ernest Wallis, PhD. (New York: Charles Scribner's Sons, 1911), Vol. 5, 423.
25 (Scrivener, A Plain introduction to the New Testament Textual Criticism 405)

In Defense of the Authenticity of 1 John 5:7

rejected the Comma as being part of Holy Scriptures. He wrote concerning the Comma, "It belongs not to the whole Christian church but to a single branch of it, and in early times only to one fruitful offshoot of that Branch."[26] That single branch of the church he referred to was the African church. Presently this assessment by Dr. Scrivener is being questioned.

For example, Dr. Scrivener adamantly asserted that the origin of the Old Latin text was African. But is this true?[27] Dr. Scrivener wrote, "But while it must be admitted, on grounds simply philological, that Africa was the parent of the Old Latin Bible..."[28] Then he seemed to contradict himself by going on to say, "Nearly all the chief manuscripts were discovered in regions in north Italy."[29] That is, all of the chief Old Latin manuscripts were discovered in northern Italy. If this is not a contradiction, then what will we make of what is said? Could it be that the Bible of the African church came out of Italy? Or did the Bible of Italy come out of Africa? Or better still, does this shoot holes in his dividing the church into separate branches or families?

Scholars are questioning Dr. Scrivener's assessment.[30] If their assessment is true, then it is without question that the Comma was not limited to one fruitful branch of the church, as the School of Higher Textual Criticism affirms. As it was earlier stated, nearly all of the Old Latin manuscripts of 1 John were found in northern Italy. Also keep in mind that it was the pope who commissioned Jerome to produce the Vulgate to replace the Old Latin Scriptures, which then

---

26 (Scrivener, Six Lectures on the Text of the New Testament 206)
27 (Scrivener, A Plain introduction to the New Testament Textual Criticism 44)
28 (Scrivener, Six Lectures on the Text of the New Testament 99)
29 (Scrivener, Six Lectures on the Text of the New Testament 99)
30 (Scrivener, A Plain introduction to the New Testament Textual Criticism 44)

were being used by the churches under papal rule. What is startling is how men are blind to the obvious!

The writer does not like to refer to the different branches of the church. This too is an invention of the School of Higher Textual Criticism. These men have artificially divided the church into three separate branches–Eastern, African, and Western. Each of these so–called branches was given an equal witness. Others since then have sought to make the divisions even greater. However, such divisions are utterly foolish. The church is not divided. She is one body, having, "One Lord, one faith, one baptism, One God and Father of all, who is above all, and through all, and in you all" (Eph. 4:5–6). Christians are sojourners on this earth, a people of the Book. It is then absolutely criminal to seek to divide the church into different branches. More will be said on this later.

It is admitted that Erasmus in his first two editions of the Greek New Testament omitted the Comma. However, he did not omit it in his Latin edition of the New Testament published in 1521. Nor did he omit it in his later three editions of his Greek New Testament. He later argued in favor of the Comma from the Latin witnesses. He said, "It could not have been in the Latin manuscripts if it were not translated from the Greek."[31] This is a compelling argument that should be given some thoughtful consideration. Translators translate!

There is no question that Erasmus had a Greek manuscript from which he read the Comma. He was too much a scholar to do otherwise. Some argue that Erasmus read the Comma from the manuscript Britannicus. This may be questioned, but it should never be implied that Erasmus translated the Comma from the Latin Vulgate, as

---

31 Erasmus, *Erasmus of Christendom.* Ed. Roland H Bainton (New York: Charles Scribner's & Son,1969), 137.

In Defense of the Authenticity of 1 John 5:7

not a few have suggested. Stunica, the chief editor of the Complutensian Greek text, entered into a controversy with Erasmus on this very matter. He chided Erasmus because he did not translate the Comma from the Latin as they did.[32] (The Complutensian Greek New Testament was produced in Alicia, Spain, in 1517 and was authorized by the pope.) It is interesting that they too did not omit the Comma. They were too scholarly to do otherwise.

One thing is apparent; Erasmus did not translate the Comma from the Dublin Manuscript, as many of late have suggested. Those who affirm such are seeking to discredit the Trinitarian passage. Men making such claims are not honest or are misinformed. Anyone who would compare the disputed text in Erasmus's later three editions of the Greek New Testament with that of the Dublin passage would discover there are some glaring differences. Those who ignore these differences and affirm otherwise are not honest with either the Erasmus text or with the Dublin text, for the differences between them are considerable.

Time would fail us to mention the many other external witnesses who may be summoned to testify in favor of the Johanneum Comma. The writer does not wish to labor the reader with a long list of references. However, witnesses need to be summoned. For example, of the church Fathers, we have Athenagorus quoting it as well as Tertullian and Cyprian. Of the Post–Nicene Fathers, Augustine cited 1 John 5:7.[33] Priscillian is also known to quote the passage. Priscillian was beheaded in AD 385 by the Catholic Church because they said he was a "heretic." They accused him of Manichaeism. But the discovery of some of his writings has

---

32 (Scrivener, A Plain introduction to the New Testament Textual Criticism 405)

33 Nestle-Aland, *Greek New Testament*, 13th Ed. (American Bible Society, New York, 1927), 205.

proven this accusation to be false. He (or Bishop Instantius, his follower) cited 1 John 5:7 in the *Liber Apologeticus* (Chapter 4).[34] All of these witnesses predate the tenth–century manuscript that has the Comma in the margin. As for translations, it is in the Peshitto that is the most revered Bible of Syria. Of late, there are those who propose that the New Testament was first written in Syrian and later translated into the Greek. Whether this is true or not, the fact remains that the Peshitto is a very early witness to the Comma. However, the writer is of the persuasion that the New Testament was first penned in Greek and very soon thereafter was translated into Latin and Syrian. But besides these disagreements, the Peshitto is a very early witness of the Comma. This one translation of the Scriptures alone is a very powerful witness to the validity of the Comma.

Then there are the Slavic Bibles. These too have the Comma in their translations of the Scriptures. This is not to mention the Russian Bible, which also has the Comma. How did the Comma enter into these translations if it were not in the Greek Bible? After all, these translations were translated from the Greek manuscripts.

Another witness summoned on behalf of the Comma is the Celtic Bible. The history of the Celts is very interesting indeed. In 2 Timothy 4:21, we are introduced to three people who were in Rome with Paul before he was executed by Nero. These names were Pudens, Linus, and Claudia. Pudens married Claudia. It is believed that they were converted under the apostle Paul's preaching while in Rome. They are said to have been from Wales and from families of nobility. Other Roman soldiers who also were Welshmen were converted at this time. Together these saints are said to have taken the Gospel to their people in Wales. We learn

---

34 Bruce M. Metzger, *A commentary on the Greek New Testament*, 2nd Ed. (American Bible Society, New York, 1993), 64.

from Tertullian that in AD 130, he sent two ministers to Britain to assist them in the work. The names of these two men are Faganus and Damianus.[35] Thus the Celtic Translation is a very strong witness dating back to the time of the apostle Paul.

Then there is the French or Gallic Bible printed in Lyons, the German Bible prior to Luther, the Telp Bible of the fourteenth century of Bohemia, and the Swiss Bible. It is interesting to note that the Swiss never accepted Luther's Bible. Then there is also the Italian Bible. All of these translations of the Scriptures contain the Comma. Neither should we think that the Bible was lost in Germany until Luther came along. The German people definitely had the Scriptures in their language long before Luther.

As for the English translations, we have the Wycliffe Bible, 1380; the Tyndale Bible, 1525; the Miles Coverdale Bible, 1535; the Matthew's Bible, 1537; the Taverner's Bible, 1539; the Great Bible, 1539; the Geneva Bible, 1557; the Bishop's Bible, 1568; and the Authorized Version, 1611. Interestingly enough, it was not until 1881 that the Comma was ever questioned. As one can readily discern, the Comma was never brought into question by any of the earlier English translators. They never doubted its authenticity. It was only brought into suspicion in 1881! Thus, over a period of more than five hundred years, the Comma was universally accepted without any reservations. Were men without light until then?

It was in the Waldenses' Bible that Helvidius, the Waldensian scholar, charged Jerome with corrupting the Scriptures. And as for the Waldenses, they date back to AD 120. They were under relentless persecution by the Church of Rome. Not only were these people destroyed but also their

---

35 G. H. Orchard, Essay by J. R. Graves, *History of Baptist* (Texarkana, TX, Bogard Press, 1987), xxi.

writings, their Bibles, and their libraries. Their copies of the Sacred Scriptures that have survived are extremely few and are not very good copies at that. However, they testified to the authenticity of the questioned passage.

Enough is stated to show that sufficient external evidence exists testifying on behalf of the Comma. These witnesses should not be overlooked. They are overwhelming. Who can ignore the early church father Cyprian (AD 200–258) and those mentioned before him in the second century? And how can we ignore the Post–Nicene Fathers who quote the Comma? Furthermore, who would dare ignore the early translations of the Scriptures that contain the Comma? Some of these translations date back to the middle of the second century. This is not to mention the Waldenses' testimony to the authenticity of the questioned passage. Those who know anything of the history of the Kingdom of God know that these people were the true light bearers in the West.

It is well known that the editors of the Authorized Version consulted with Geneva while laboring on the translation of the Authorized Version. But many are not aware that they consulted with three Waldensian scholars. With the deaths of Calvin and Beza, their successors were Leger, Diodati of Italy, and Olivetan of France. All three of these men were Waldenses with whom they conferred. As for Diodati, he gave the Italians their Bible. And as for Olivetan, he gave the French their Bible. None of these men questioned the Comma. As stated earlier, the Comma was in the Waldensian Bible!

Benjamin Warfield mentions the translators of the Authorized Version consulting with Waldensians. He wrote, "It is known that among modern versions they consulted was an Italian[sic], and though no name is mentioned, there cannot be room for doubt that it was the elegant translation made with great ability from the original Scriptures by

Giovanni Diodati, which had only recently, (1607) appeared in Geneva."[36] The Waldenses, in coming to Geneva, made Geneva a light bearer for over one hundred years. And as for Calvin, he was no doubt related to Leger, as both of their families were from the Valley of St. Martin, a Waldensian community.

In light of this great host of witnesses, the Comma must be retained. It was retained in all of Christendom from its inception. The argument against it is that it was not as strong as it should be in the Greek manuscripts. This is true, but is not the fact that our Lord preserved the Johanneum Comma in the Greek text as well as in the Latin Church a testimony to His faithfulness? And as for the Greek Church, she has always retained the Trinitarian passage without question.

> Thy Word is a lamp to my feet, A light to my Path alway, To guide and to save me from sin, And show me the heave'nly way. Thy Word have I hid in my heart That I might not sin against thee; That I might not sin, that I might not sin, Thy Word have I hid in my heart.
>
> For ever, O Lord is thy Word Established and fixed on high; Thy Faithfulness unto all men Abideth for ever nigh. Thy Word have I hid in my heart That I might not sin against thee; That I might not sin, that I might not sin, Thy Word have I hid in my heart.
>
> ––Psalm 119:11, adapted by E. O. Sellers, 1908

---

[36] Benjamin B. Warfield, of Princeton University, Collections of Opinions and Reviews, Vol. 2 (New York: Oxford Press, 1932), 99.

Chapter 2

The Witness of the Church

There is yet another external witness on behalf of the Johanneum Comma that was touched upon briefly in the previous chapter. This witness is seldom, if ever, taken into consideration. At least it was never taken into consideration by those who produced the Revised Version. If they had, and there is no evidence that they did, they would never have questioned the Trinitarian passage. This is because the church universal and throughout the ages faithfully testified to the authenticity of the Comma. (Note the previous chapter and the appendix.)

The saints in every century, regardless if they were African, Asian, or even European, embraced the Trinitarian passage without reservation. It was part of their creeds and confessions. It was quoted by the Ante–Nicene Fathers as well as the Post–Nicene Fathers. It was found in their various translations of the Scriptures. All of this indicates, from the earliest dating until 1881, that the Trinitarian passage was never brought into question. The Comma was universally accepted by the church until the Revision Committee brought it into question. And even then the church never accepted the Revision Committee's verdict on the Comma as it continued undisputed in the Received Greek Text and thus in the Authorized Version.

To put it as simply as possible, the Johanneum Comma was unquestionably accepted by the church for 1,800 years! Why now is it, after all this time, questioned? It is because ungodly men subtly infiltrated the church. Some of these men became powerful members on the Revision Committee. Now their opportunity had arrived. These powerful members on the committee were able to do what they could have never done before: mutilate the Scriptures.

They knew the outrage that would come if they removed the Comma altogether from the Sacred Text. Therefore, they placed the Comma in brackets, as they did with many other passages of the Scriptures. They waited for a more favorable opportunity when they could remove the Johanneum Comma altogether from the Scriptures. From the very beginning, when the Revised Version of the Scriptures was presented to the saints, it was met with outrage.

It took well over a hundred years before any members of the Christian community ever accepted the Revised Version or the American Standard Version of the Scriptures. At first, the liberals openly welcomed it and hailed it as a masterful work. However, to this day there still remains a host of Christians who reject the new versions of the Bible. The saints, as those before them, are not ready to allow anyone to remove a single passage from the Bible they cherish. Hence, there still remains the continual witness of the church testifying to the validity of the disputed passage. This is not to imply that the church of our Lord Jesus Christ was never plagued with heretical writings, for there were many heretics who labored to corrupt the Holy Scriptures. These men never ceased with time. They are still active among us.

However, those men and their writings are not to be taken into the equation. Those men were outside of the pales of the church. They were and are the enemies of our Lord Jesus Christ. Who then in their right mind would look to such men and their heretical writings and cite them as evidences in corrupting the Word of God? No one in their right mind would dare to do that!

However, it is quite apparent that the men who revised the Authorized Version of the Scriptures did exactly that! Is this not evident in that they never separated those corrupt manuscripts, such as the Vaticanus and the Sinaiticus, from the Sacred Documents in composing their Revised Version of the Scriptures? Instead of separating the heretical writings from the pure, they lumped them all together. A greater crime was how they heavily leaned upon those two corrupt documents in giving us the Revised Version. Those two manuscripts were given more weight as witnesses than the pure, unadulterated manuscripts of later date that the churches used!

In spite of the powerful testimony of the church on behalf of the Comma, those men insisted upon removing the Comma from the Holy Scriptures. The main reason given for the removal of the Comma was that it is only found in nine Greek manuscripts. Four of them have the Comma in the margin, and five of them have it in the text itself. Furthermore, the oldest manuscript that has the Comma is tenth century, and then it is in the margin. This is the central argument set forth by those who reject the Trinitarian passage. Also, any manuscript tenth century or later was dismissed or given very little weight.

In the light of the faithful witness of the church throughout the ages, are the above arguments viable for removing the Comma from the Bible? It is beyond a doubt that the church held to the Comma throughout the ages.

In Defense of the Authenticity of 1 John 5:7

Are we then to ignore the faithful witness of the church? Are we to lean wholly upon the fact that there were so few witnesses in surviving Greek manuscripts to give any credence to the Johanneum Comma? Well let's take a look at their argument for a moment.

If the church had not held to the Trinitarian passage until the tenth century, then the critics may have had an argument for removing this passage from the Holy Bible. But this is not the case at all. The Comma was well attested to by the church, which is an indisputable fact. It is witnessed to by both the Ante–Nicene and Post–Nicene Fathers. There is also the witness of the early translations of the Scriptures found throughout the world as well as throughout the centuries. These witnesses precede the earliest extant Greek manuscripts that we have in our possession. So we ask, "What justification did and do these contemporary textual critics have in removing 1 John 5:7 from the Bible?" Absolutely none! Even though a tenth–century manuscript is the oldest Greek manuscript we have containing the Comma, it is without question that the church had always held to the Trinitarian passage from its inception.

What then are we to make of the oldest manuscript that contains 1 John 5:7 being tenth century? The simple conclusion is that the oldest manuscript we have containing the Comma is tenth century. This is all that we can conclude from this fact! This does not prove anything more than that. It does not prove that the Comma was absent prior to that date and time. It simply means the oldest manuscript that has survived that contains the Comma is tenth century. This is all that it means!

What do we make of only nine Greek manuscripts having the Comma? The only concrete conclusion we can arrive at is that we only have nine extant Greek manuscripts that contain the Comma. This is all we can safely conclude from the facts. We may wonder why only nine Greek manuscripts have the Comma, but we cannot question its validity because so few manuscripts contain it. To imply that it was not in the Original Autograph is mere speculation since the church always attested to it.

Let us pause for a moment and consider the critics' arguments for removing the Comma. But this time, let us consider it from another perspective. For an example, the writer has but one photograph of his mother. That was all that has survived. Also, this photograph was taken when she was fifty years of age. However, he has many photographs of his family. Many of these photographs are of a much later date. What conclusion are we to draw from these photographs?

One is that his mother did not exist until she was fifty years of age. This is a physical impossibility, so it shall be dismissed. However, there is another conclusion that may be drawn; she was not a member of the family until she was fifty years of age. She then must be his stepmother, rather than his biological mother. This is a reasonable conclusion. However, such a conclusion has to be dismissed in light of external evidences. These witnesses who testify to her being his biological mother are his immediate family, as well as that of the extended family. Then there are other witnesses as well, such as marriage licenses, birth certificates, and baptismal certificates, to mention a few. In light of the preponderance of these witnesses, the only conclusion one can rightly draw is that she is indeed his mother.

It is ludicrous to assume in light of the external evidences, because there is only one photograph of the writer's mother, and that of a late date, that she is not his biological mother. All that can be rightly determined is that he has but one photograph of his mother and that of a late date. So, in like manner, that is all we can state concerning the Comma. All

In Defense of the Authenticity of 1 John 5:7

we can rightly conclude is that the oldest Greek manuscript we have in our possession that contains the Comma is from the tenth century. Does this mean that the Comma did not exist as Scripture until then? In light of the preponderance of witnesses of the church throughout the ages, such a claim is absurd.

Speculations cannot and must not be admitted as evidence. Therefore, it is neither scientific nor is it safe to conclude that the Johanneum Comma does not belong in Holy Scripture. If we do come to such a conclusion, then we are faced with a greater problem. How are we to explain the testimony of the church on its behalf? It is definitely not safe to assume that the Comma was introduced into the Scriptures through some pious scribe in the tenth century. Such a thought in light of the external evidences is absurd!

The question that now confronts us is how did the revisers justify themselves in removing the Comma from the Scriptures when the church throughout the centuries testified to it? The answer to this question is found in the methods they employed in revising the Scriptures. From the onset, they sought to rediscover the Original Autograph. They scoffed at the thought of divine preservation of the Scriptures.[37] Thus they labored using the same methods anyone would apply in seeking to restore the original of any profane writing. Therefore, the testimony of the church is not to be taken into the equation. All that counts are manuscripts, and the older they are, the more authoritative they are, regardless of their corruption!

Of these men who revised the Scriptures, R. L. Dabney wrote:

---

37 Dean Burgon and Jay P. Green, *An introduction to Textual Criticism*, Vol. 1 (Lafayette, IN: Sovereign Grace Trust Fund, 1990), xiv.

> They dissect the evangelists, epistles and prophets, just as they do Homer or Vedas. They have never felt that declaration of our Savior: "The words that I speak unto you, they are spirit, and they are life." The response which is made by the profoundest intuitions of the human heart and conscience, quickened by the Spirit, to these Lively Oracles, immediately avouching them as the words of the Creator of the human soul, is unnoticed by these critics. They propose to settle the authenticity or falsehood of the (Biblical) records by antiquarian processes only, similar by which Niebuhr proposed to test the legends of early Rome, or Wolf the genuineness of the Homeric epics.[38]

These were no mere exaggerations made by Dabney. He understood their methods well. The men laboring on the Revision Committee denied the preservation of the Scriptures. This led them in a search for the Scriptures. And after they had completed their work, they presented to the church a Bible that they could not uphold to be inerrant. This is clearly stated in so many words in the opening sentence of the introduction of Westcott and Hort's book entitled, *Introduction to the New Testament in the Original Greek*. They wrote, "The edition is an attempt to present exactly the original words of the New Testament, so far as they can now be determined from surviving documents."[39]

Notice the Revision Committee made "an attempt" *to present the exact words of the New Testament.* In other words, they are saying the church never possessed the inerrant Word of God. And they also confessed they never fully

---

38 (Dean Burgon and Jay P. Green xv)
39 (Brooke F. Westcott and Fenton J. A. Hort 3)

recovered the Original Autograph. However, they did make an attempt to do so. All they did was to make an attempt!

Also note how they said the same thing again but in a different way. They confessed they had recovered the Scriptures *"so far as they can now be determined from surviving documents."*[40] What are they saying? They are saying they are not sure that they have recovered all the surviving documents necessary to produce an inerrant Bible. There is room for more discoveries in the future. Thus we have been given a Bible that contains the Word of God whereas before we had the Bible that is the Word of God!

Not only were their methods wrong, but many of these men who handled the Scriptures were also in utter darkness. Their theology was heretical. The liberals and Unitarians on the committee corrupted the Sacred Scriptures by fitting the Scriptures to their theology. For example, passages that affirmed the Trinity and the deity of our Lord were either altered or removed. 1 John 5:7 and 1 Timothy 3:16 were never questioned by anyone in the pales of the Christian church until the Revision Committee of 1881 came along. Yet they changed the key words of 1 Timothy 3:16 from "…God was manifest in the flesh…" to read "he" or "who" "was manifest in the flesh."

Of this change Dr. Vance Smith commented:

> The old reading has been pronounced untenable by the Revisers, as it has long been known to be by all careful students of the New Testament … It is another example of the facility with which the ancient copiers could introduce the word "God" into their manuscripts – a reading which was the natural result of the growing tendency in the early Christian times to look upon the

---

40 (Brooke F. Westcott and Fenton J. A. Hort 3)

> humble Teacher as the incarnate Word, and therefore as "God manifested in flesh."[41]

Is this not blasphemy? The reason the two Revision Committees removed the Comma from the Scriptures was not because of the lack of evidence on its behalf. The reason they removed the Comma from the Scriptures was because of the godless methods they employed as well as the corrupt minds of the men employing those methods. There were men on these Revision Committees who actually denied the fundamental doctrine of the Christian faith, the deity of our Lord and the Holy Trinity.

Therefore, the fundamental reason the Comma was removed from Scripture was because there were heretics on these committees. However, at the same time there were some honest men also on the Revision Committee. But these men were led astray by powerful personalities such as Dr. Westcott, Dr. Hort, Dr. Vance Smith, Dean Stanley, Bishop Tirlwall, Dr. Moulton, and Dr. Moberly, to mention a few.[42] These men mentioned had no regard to the faithful witness of our Lord Jesus Christ through His Church. Through their craftiness under the guise of scholarship, they succeeded in corrupting the Scriptures. They succeeded in removing the Comma. But they had not succeeded in extinguishing the Light!

> The blind guides still lead the blind.
> A sad affair not altered by time.
> O may such guides ne'er be mine!
> Thy Word's my guide, Lord I am Thine!

---

41 (Fuller, True or False 26-27)
42 (Fuller, Which Bible 296-297)

CHAPTER 3

Why the Comma in Few Greek Manuscripts

The question may be asked, why is it that there are so few Greek manuscripts that testify on behalf of the Comma? If the Comma is so strongly attested to by the churches, one would assume that it would be more prominent in the Byzantine manuscripts. But this is not the case. However, it is without question that the Trinitarian passage is very strongly attested to in the Latin manuscripts. So the question remains, why wasn't the Johanneum Comma more pronounced in the manuscripts of the Greek Church?

The question that is posed is not designed to bring into doubt the certainty of the Trinitarian passage. It is designed to challenge the mind of the reader to inquire into those reasons why the Comma is not as pronounced as it should be in the Greek manuscripts. It is the purpose of the writer at this time to explore those reasons. As for the omission of the Comma in many of the Greek manuscripts, there are several historical events with which the reader should become familiar, in particular, the early history of the Greek Church. This would help him or her understand the problem at hand. There were three major historical events that led to the present controversy. These events must not be overlooked. They are pertinent to the question at hand, for nothing ever happens in a vacuum!

The first major historical event that should be taken into consideration is the reign of Emperor Diocletian. He reigned from AD 284 to 312. In the last ten years of his reign, he launched a horrendous attack against the Church. The emperor was determined to stamp out Christianity from the face of the earth. The Christian faith was rapidly growing, making its way into almost every home, palace, and even the Roman Senate. Christians were also found in Caesar's household! Why, even Diocletian's wife, Prisca, and his daughter, Valeria, had become Christians. This is not to mention many of the eunuchs in the palace who were converted to the faith. At this time, Christianity was working as leaven permeating the entire Roman Empire. Thus Diocletian, in the last ten years of his reign, dedicated himself to one end: eradicate Christianity.

Thus, from approximately AD 303 to 312, almost an entire decade, Diocletian searched out and destroyed every copy of the Holy Scriptures he could find. The reason he was determined to destroy the Sacred Scriptures was because he knew Christians were people of the Book. He knew that in order to destroy Christianity, he had to first destroy the Bible. Roman Emperors before him had discovered that putting the saints to death only fueled the fire. The more Christians they killed, the more they multiplied. Therefore, Diocletian resorted to destroying the eternal Word of God. He knew that as long as there was a copy of the Sacred Scriptures, there would be believers. So in a relentless and

In Defense of the Authenticity of 1 John 5:7

furious attack upon Christianity, Emperor Diocletian gave the orders to search out and destroy the Sacred Oracles.

Roman soldiers broke into homes and churches, searching, seizing, and destroying every copy of the Holy Writ that they could find. If the saints did not turn the Scriptures over to them to be destroyed, they were put to death. In those days, many saints were martyred. They would rather die than turn over the Holy Oracles into the hands of men to be destroyed. However, there were the timid and fearful who handed over the Scriptures into the hands of the enemy. They did so in order that their lives might be spared. These people were called "traditores."[43] It is from this word we get our word traitors. These traitors were removed from the fellowship of the saints because they betrayed the sacred trust that God had committed unto their keeping.

Needless to say, Diocletian succeeded in destroying a tremendous amount of these copies of the Holy Bible. By AD 312, there were but a very few copies of the Scriptures that had survived. These copies of the Word of God were not so quickly replaced, as there were no printing presses in those days. We must keep in mind that the Scriptures were copied by hand. These copyists were calligraphers. They tediously labored for many days, weeks, and even months copying a single epistle of the Scriptures.

Such a work as copying the Sacred Scriptures was not done overnight. Neither were such men great in number who could fulfill the task. This is not to mention the cost involved in producing copies of the Sacred Text. The church of the Lamb of God was financially poor. As Peter and John, silver and gold she had none. Also keep in mind that in copying the Scriptures, there must be no mistakes. Each leaf

---

43 (Scrivener, Six Lectures on the Text of the New Testament 9)

had to be proofread. The task, as one can readily perceive, was enormous as well as laboriously slow.

Dr. Scrivener mentions the aftermath of the Diocletian persecution. He writes, "The result was deplorable enough, though in God's mercy the worst effects of the enemy's malice were frustrated. When the church had rest again, the volumes of the Holy Scriptures that could be gotten together were comparatively few."[44]

Many in the Latin Church fled to the mountains. This, no doubt, is the reason that almost all of the Old Italic manuscripts we have in our possession were discovered in northern Italy. But when we consider those thriving metropolises such as Constantinople, Antioch, and Alexandria, the centers of the Greek Church, this is a different story. The Greek manuscripts were easily discovered and destroyed in those places. Thus the persecution of Diocletian left the Church with a very few copies of the Scriptures. These copies that survived were copied upon inferior materials called papyrus. Papyrus did not have a long shelf life. Those that were not destroyed by malice were quickly worn out because of use. Hence the copies of the Holy Scriptures that survived would soon have to be replaced. But how this would be accomplished is another matter altogether because the Church was in a deplorable state!

This persecution was soon followed by the second malady that was even worse than the former. This was the reign of Constantine the Great. Even though he declared Christianity to be the religion of the empire, and though with his coming to power he lifted the persecutions against the saints, he was no friend to the Church, regardless of what historians may say. With Constantine coming into

---

44 (Scrivener, Six Lectures on the Text of the New Testament 9)

power, he quickly declared himself to be the head of the Church. He assumed the position of the high priest. He, as the former emperors before him, took on the title of "Pontific Maxims." By assuming this position, he usurped the position of our Lord Jesus Christ. He declared himself the high priest over the Church!

This act created another problem, for as Christianity became the religion of the empire, it ceased to be the religion of the Bible. Now for the first time, there was an unholy union of church and state. There was no distinction made between the subjects of Rome and the saints of the Most High God! To be a citizen of Rome was at the same time to be a Christian.

However, in order for the emperor to achieve his end, that is to become recognized as the head of the Church, he had to get the bishops to acknowledge him as their head. The way he sought to accomplish this was to summon the bishops in the entire empire to gather together for a council in Nicaea. He even paid their expenses in order that all might attend. This gathering is known as the First Ante-Nicene Council, which was held in AD 325. By virtue of the emperor presiding over the council, and thus over the bishops attending, he obtained his objective. He was acknowledged as the head of the Church. It was in that council the great controversy broke out over the deity of our Lord Jesus Christ. This debate became more acute in time.

At this time or shortly prior, a third factor came into play. Constantine commissioned Eusebius of Caesarea to produce fifty manuscripts of the New Testament. These were to replace those manuscripts that were destroyed during the Diocletian persecution. In light of the aftermath of the Diocletian persecution, there was a great need for copies of the Sacred Text. These copies of the Scriptures Eusebius produced were copied upon a much more substantial material called vellum. Vellum was made of animal skins and would last much longer than the Scriptures copied on papyrus. The shelf life of these new copies of the Scripture was considerably longer, and if not used, they would last indefinitely.

However, Eusebius was a student of Origen. Origen was the father of the Alexandrian school that corrupted the Scriptures in seeking to correct them. These were the copies of the Scriptures Eusebius leaned upon in producing the fifty manuscripts ordered by the emperor. Two of these manuscripts are believed to have survived to this day. These are the Vaticanus and Sinaiticus. In both of these manuscripts, the Comma is omitted. Is this of any wonder! Remember, Eusebius' mentor was Origen, who wavered between the Orthodox and Arian position concerning the Second Person of the Godhead. And this was Eusebius' position as well.

Philip Schaff writes of Origen, who "wavered between the Homo–ousian, (same in essence and thus God) orthodox, and the Homoi–ousian (like God but a lesser God) or subordinate theories, which afterwards came into sharp conflict with each other in the Arian controversy."[45]

One can see how Origen's theology gave fuel to the Arians' controversy. What is worse is that the Arians soon thereafter took over the helm of the Church. This is another event in history that is ignored. At this time, the Arians had the emperor's support. Eusebius himself was a Semi–Arian, as Origen, his mentor, if there is such a thing. Tragically, the emperor looked to Eusebius for counsel in regard to this controversy concerning the deity of our Lord. Eusebius regurgitated Origen's theology that the Son was begotten in eternity and thus a lesser God.

---

[45] (Schaff, History of the Christian Church, Vol. 2 551)

In Defense of the Authenticity of 1 John 5:7

Keep in mind that it was Eusebius who was commissioned to produce these fifty copies of the Scriptures ordered by the Emperor. Interestingly, Jerome embraced Eusebius' works in producing the Latin Vulgate! Is it any wonder that Jerome, as Eusebius before him, omitted the Comma? And is it any wonder that both produced copies of the Scriptures that the saints never accepted?

Many are under the delusion that the Arian controversy was settled in AD 325 at the time of the first Ante–Nicene Council. But nothing is further from the truth. Athanasius, who defended the deity of our Lord, may have won the day, but the war was far from being over. The emperor Constantine the Great had him exiled on five different occasions because of his opposition to Arius (the Arian Bishop), whom the emperor befriended. So the war over the deity of our Lord had never ceased. It still rages to this day and will until our Lord returns. This becomes more apparent when one considers the efforts of unscrupulous men removing the Comma from Holy Writ.

Another factor enters into the picture. Shortly thereafter, the Arian priest Eusebius of Nicomedia was promoted by Constantine the Great to be the bishop of Constantinople. Thus, the foremost leader of the Greek Church was an Arian denying, as well as opposing, the doctrine of the deity of our Lord Jesus Christ. With his promotion came the promotions of other Arian bishops over sundry congregations. However, the people in the beginning did not receive them. When the Arian bishop Arius was sent to replace Athanasius of Alexandria, who was in exile, the city rioted and sent the heretic bishop fleeing from the city. This infuriated the Emperor Constantine, but he found himself helpless to change the situation except by the shedding of blood, which he was not at the time willing to do.

Keep in mind that at this time, the Greek Church had very few copies of the Sacred Scriptures. The copies of the Scriptures that were being produced by Constantine were corrupt. The Comma was omitted. Arians rose to power shortly after the aftermath of the Diocletian persecution. Origen's influence on the Scriptures was predominant at the time. The Church also had fallen from her pristine glory as she now entered into an unholy union with the state. And even worse, Arian bishops were at the helm supported by the emperor. The Orthodox bishops were denied support unless they conformed to the whims of the emperor. Hence, they struggled and were left to fend for themselves.

Thus, from at least AD 330 (or earlier) until about AD 379, a period of half a century, the Arians had total control of the Greek Church. With such heretics at the helm empowered by Arian emperors, it is not hard to discern why the Comma was omitted from so many of the early Greek manuscripts. The raging fanaticism of the Arian Emperor Valens (AD 364–378) is but one example of such emperors who were cruel and oppressive to the saints. Nevertheless, there were restraints upon them as to how far they might go. There were still a few true believers who contended for the faith. It could also be said of them, "Never in the field of human conflict was so much owed by so many to so few."[46] The Trinitarian passage was challenged during the latter part of the fourth century, and ferocious battles raged around it.

The war over the deity of our Lord was quite apparent, as there were strong debates between the Arians and Gregory of Nazianzus, who in AD 379 was appointed bishop in Constantinople. Up to this time, the Arians held the upper hand in supplying copies of the New Testament to the

---

46 Stephen Mansfield, *Never Give In*, (Ny, Ny: Hyperion, 2003) 384

churches. They were the ones who were supported out of the emperor's coffers. The true church was in desperate need of the Scriptures. They also lacked the financial support the Arians had to produce copies of the Word of God. Furthermore, the copies they produced were upon inferior materials, such as papyrus which had a very short shelf life, especially with use. Not only were the Orthodox bishops without support, but they were also persecuted by these Arian emperors. Therefore, it should not be surprising that the Comma is not as pronounce as we would like it in the early Greek manuscripts.

At this time, it should also be acknowledged that the true church of our Lord Jesus Christ had departed from the mainline church of which Constantine declared himself to be the head. The familiar cry first uttered by Tertullian was again resounded, "What does Caesar have to do with the church?" The saints at this time began to slowly migrate into the wilderness. Furthering their struggles, Constantine's son was even more oppressive as a ruler than his father. For the next half a century, there would be the struggle in the Greek Church over the doctrine of the deity of our Lord.

But in AD 378, the tide began to turn. The orthodox Emperor Gratian came into power. He then appointed Theodosius, who was also orthodox in his theology, as emperor in the east. With the ascension of Theodosius, Gregory of Nazianzus was elevated to be the bishop of Constantinople. This took place in year AD 379. But the situation did not change overnight; there were still long and hard battles to be fought. By this time, most of the people and bishops who were installed in the churches were Arians.

Philip Schaff mentions the promotion of Gregory to the See in Constantinople and the challenges he faced. He writes, "But Providence had appointed him yet a great work and an exalted position in the Eastern capital of the empire. In the year 379 he was called to the pastoral charge by the orthodox church in Constantinople, which under the oppressive reign of Arianism, was reduced to a feeble handful; and he was exhorted by several worthy bishops to accept the call."[47]

Gregory did accept the call and ministered to a very small congregation. But it must not be overlooked that this faithful few lived in the capital of the empire and the center of the Greek Church that professed to be Christian. Even though an orthodox emperor ascended to the throne, and a noted orthodox theologian was appointed over the See of Constantinople, there were still hard battles to be fought. Acknowledging the opposition Gregory had to overcome, Schaff writes, "Once the Arian populace even stormed his church by night, desecrated the altar, mixed the holy wine with blood, and Gregory but barely escaped the fury of common women and monks, who were armed with clubs and stones."[48] As the reader can readily see, the Arian heresy was deeply rooted throughout the Byzantine Empire.

In spite of such obstacles, Gregory established a great congregation in the city. The Church Anastasia was established with great success. Anastasia means "resurrection," which was a fitting title, as it was symbolic of the dawning of the resurrection of the church. Light was breaking forth, scattering the darkness, and by AD 381, the church was beginning to grow. During this time, Gregory strongly contended for the Comma that was rightfully restored to the Scriptures. To this day, it is unquestionably embraced by the Greek Orthodox Church.

Nevertheless, the reader must not think that the Arianism plague was quickly stamped out. It took another two centuries to overcome the havoc of those first fifty

---

47 (Schaff, History of the Christian Church, Vol. 3 917)
48 (Schaff, History of the Christian Church, Vol. 3 917)

years when the Arians controlled the church. They were very evangelistic, evangelizing the Goths, Vandals, and Slavic nations, as well as those nations in the East. With the marriage of the state to the church, all in the empire were to embrace Christianity. This union would explain how Arianism permeated the Empire. It would also explain why the Trinitarian passage was omitted in so many of the early translations in those tongues. However, in time the damage of the Arians was overcome and the Greek Orthodox Church came out the stronger for it.

An equally interesting event is that when the Reformation was taking place in the West, Cyril I, better known as Cyril Lucaris, Patriarch of Constantinople, sought to reform the Greek Orthodox Church. Cyril Lucaris was born in 1572 and was murdered in 1638. He was murdered before he could accomplish his work. But before he was murdered, this brilliant textual critic translated the Greek Bible into the common Greek language so that every Greek could read the Scriptures for him or herself. What is of equal interest is that we find 1 John 5:7 in the Contemporary Greek Bible even as it is in the Authorized Version.

No one would deny that Cyril Lucaris was an exceptional scholar. Neither would anyone deny that he used the Byzantine manuscripts to translate the Scriptures into the contemporary Greek language. He also had access to other manuscripts since he was a notable textual critic. Thus being so esteemed and, furthermore, well acquainted with the history of the Greek manuscripts, he did not find the Comma to be a problem simply because so few of those manuscripts contained it.

What is also arresting is that the Greek Orthodox Church to this day uses only the King James or the New King James Bible when using an English version of the New Testament. They will not endorse any of the other

English translations. This should astound the reader because the English–speaking world for the most part rejects the Comma as well as the Authorized Version! But this is not so with the Greek Orthodox Church. The Greek Orthodox Church rejects all of these new translations of the Scriptures produced from the Critical Greek New Testament. This discrepancy in itself speaks volumes! To this, the reader should give some serious thought!

However, the English–speaking world continually refers to the Greek manuscripts, placing great emphasis on what the Greek text says. But at the same time, they have rejected the Greek Bible of the Greek Church! This, in itself, is a contradiction. Should not those who use the Critical Greek Text, instead of saying, "This is what the Greek says," say, "This is what the *Critical* Greek text says?" They are misleading if they do not. After all, they are not using the Greek Bible that was always used by the Greek Orthodox Church, but rather, they are using one of their own making!

As for the Greek Church, she still uses the Byzantine manuscripts, even as all the churches had until 1881. When men say, "The Greek Bible says thus and thus," the hearer should inquire, "To which Greek Bible are you referring? Is it the Critical Greek Bible, which is a strange concoction put together by a few unscrupulous men, or are you referring to the Word of God that was handed down to us through Our Lord Jesus and His apostles?"

To ask another question, why does the English–speaking world for the most part have a problem with the Johanneum Comma? Critics reject the Comma mainly on grounds that it is not as pronounced as they would like it to be in the Greek manuscripts. Is this a legitimate argument in light of the historical facts? Or is this an excuse to mutilate the Holy Bible in order to have men place their confidence in the so–called scholars rather than upon the Holy Scriptures given and preserved by God? Are we returning to the Dark Ages where popes and scholars speak with absolute authority and the Scriptures are obscured? God forbid!

Surely a reasonable person would give some consideration as to why so few Greek manuscripts have the Comma. Also, the reader should give some thought as to why the Greek Orthodox Church unequivocally accepts the Comma. Can it be because they are well acquainted with their history? Can it be because they suffered fighting the long, hard battles against the Arians, and through much persecution and suffering, they finally emerged the victors? Thank God that they are not ready to concede their hard-won victory to some outlandish assumptions made by these pseudo-scholars! And we would do well to do the same as they.

> The heav'ns declare thy glory; In ev'ry star thy wisdom shines; But when our eyes behold thy Word, We read thy Name in fairer lines.
>
> The rolling sun, the changing light, And nights and days, thy pow'r confess; But the blest volume thou hast writ Reveals thy justice and thy grace.
>
> Sun, moon, and stars convey thy praise Round the whole earth, and never stand So when thy truth began its race, It touched and glanced on ev'ry land.
>
> Nor shall thy spread gospel rest Till through the world thy Truth has run; Till Christ has all the nations blessed that see the light, or feel the sun. Amen.

Thy noblest wonders here we view
In souls renewed, and sin forgiv'n:

Lord, cleanse my sins, my soul renew,
And make thy Word my guide to heav'n.

–Isaac Watts, 1719, from Psalm 19

Chapter 4

The Internal Witness

At this time, we shall consider the "internal witness" that testifies on behalf of the authenticity of the Comma. By "internal witness," it is understood to be an appeal to the witness of the Scriptures themselves. Regardless of what the critics may say in denying the authenticity of the Comma, they cannot refute the internal evidence, that is, if they are honest with the Scriptures. The reading of the Scriptures in the original language demands without any equivocation the acceptance of the Comma.

For an example, in reading 1 John 5:7 one cannot help but detect the apostle's personal stamp upon the text. This is perceived by the title given to our Lord. He addresses the Second Person of the Trinity as "the Word." This name or title by which the apostle presents our Lord to the reader is definitely and uniquely characteristic of John and John alone. No other writer in the New Testament addresses our Lord by this title. Furthermore, we only find this title, "the Word," seven times in the entire New Testament: twice in the Gospel of John, twice in this letter of 1John, and three times in the Revelation.

It seems that if this passage were inserted into the text in the tenth century as it is assumed, then it would have most likely read, "the Father, the Son and the Holy Ghost." What is interesting is that the Church Fathers loosely quoted this passage in this manner. Cyprian for one quoted the passage as "the Father, the Son and the Holy Ghost." If this passage were added by some unknown scribe in the tenth century, no doubt he would have written it as Cyprian had. But he did not. He copied it as the apostle wrote it. This name of our Lord, "the Word," without question, bears the apostle's seal upon the Comma. Although this might be questioned, yet one finds this reasoning hard to ignore.

Secondly, the Comma must be accepted because of grammatical linguistic rules and the sentence structure of the language. When the grammatical rules of basic Greek grammar are considered, there is, by necessity, the inclusion of the Comma. If we are to make any sense of the eighth verse, which the School of Higher Textual Critics retains without suspicion, then the seventh verse, by necessity, must also be retained. However, if the seventh verse is omitted, then the eighth verse, by necessity, must also be omitted. In essence, these two passages stand and fall together. So with that said, let us consider the grammatical witness.

In the Greek language, as in any foreign language, the articles, adjectives, participles, and nouns must all be in agreement as they relate to each other in any particular sentence. They must not only agree in gender but also in number. This is a fundamental grammatical rule. A student who has studied a foreign language is familiar with this grammatical principle.

So then, if a noun is masculine in a sentence, then the articles, adjectives, and participles in relationship to that

In Defense of the Authenticity of 1 John 5:7

noun or nouns must also be masculine. The same is true if the nouns are either feminine or neuter. There cannot be the mixture of the gender of nouns, adjectives, and participles in any given sentence. To mix them would be a gross violation of the basic grammatical rules of the language. Furthermore, to mix genders of nouns, participles and adjective would only produce confusion. If such a mixture is found, then there must be an explanation for it.

With this stated, let us now consider the passage that is in question. If the Trinitarian passage is omitted, how are we to explain the masculine adjective, "τρεις" (three), the masculine article "οι" (the plural), as well as the masculine participle "μαρτυρουντες" (bear witness) in the eighth verse of this fifth chapter? The adjective, article, and the participle are all masculine. The problem arises when we consider the mixture of the masculine with neuter substantives which immediately follow. The three nouns that follow are "*the spirit, and the water, and the blood*" which are all neuter. As the reader can readily see, there is no agreement between these nouns with the masculine article, adjective, and participle that precedes them; they stand in opposition to them. Immediately, one should detect that there is a serious grammatical problem if the Comma is omitted.

The masculine adjective "three," and the masculine article "the" with the masculine participle "bear witness" (or record) of verse eight, is only understood by the attraction of the three witnesses of verse seven which are masculine. It is the Father and the Word and the Holy Ghost of the previous verse that explains the masculine adjective, article and participle in verse eight.

Therefore, insisting that the seventh verse is to be omitted creates confusion. What explanation would we have for the masculine adjective, article and participle in verse eight? Keep in mind that "the spirit, and the water, and the blood" are in opposition to the three bearing witness in the earth. Hence, in light of elementary rule of grammar, by necessity there must be the inclusion of the Comma. It is only by the force of attraction of verse seven that the participle phrase in verse eight is masculine.

However, those that oppose the inclusion of 1 John 5:7 have their explanation. They argue that the participle phrase in 1 John 5:8 is masculine because *"the spirit, and the water, and the blood"* are symbolic of the person of our Lord Jesus. Therefore, the masculine adjective, article and participle are used with the three neuter substantives *(the spirit, and the water, and the blood).* Although this may sound good, is this explanation warranted?

If this is the explanation for the masculine participle phrase preceding the neuter substantives in verse eight, then we are faced with another problem. We are compelled to inquire, how is it in verse eight that *"the Spirit, and the water, and the blood"* are symbolic of our Lord Jesus and in verse six they are not? Is there not an inconsistency here? If *"the Spirit, and the water, and the blood"* are understood to be *"the Spirit, and the water, and the blood"* in verse six, it seems that they are also to be understood in the same way in verse eight.

Also, if the Spirit in verse eight is the Holy Spirit as in verse six, then how is the Holy Spirit symbolic of our Lord? He is a distinct Person in the Trinity. We do not deny that the Three are One. However, the Holy Ghost is a distinct Person even as the Father and the Son are distinct Persons. Furthermore, we are told that three and not one are bearing witness in earth. To insist that *"the Spirit, and the water, and the blood"* are symbolic of our Lord would reduce the three witnesses to one. To pursue this course would, therefore, only lead to more confusion.

Again, if the apostle's intention was to refer to our Lord Jesus in verse eight symbolically as *"the Spirit, and the water, and the blood,"* would he not have symbolized *"the Spirit, and the water, and the blood"* to mean the same in verse six? But he did not do that. Hence to insist that *"the Spirit, and the water, and the blood"* in verse eight is symbolic of our Lord would be inconsistent with the apostle's writing. Context is important. It should also be observed that there is a parallelism between verses seven and eight that would require *"the Spirit, and the water, and the blood"* to be the subjects of "οι μαρτυρουντες" in verse eight (the ones bearing witness). The masculine plural participle (in verse eight) is used because of the parallelism with verse seven and this by "attraction" to the same participle as is used in the seventh verse. This parallelism is a characteristic of John's style in writing. Consider the example in verse nine "…the witness of men, the witness of God…" And again in verse ten; "He that believeth…he that believeth not…", etc. This is the very reason that the full form of verse seven must be authentic.[49]

However, the above argument is not new. Gregory of Nazianzus, also known as Gregory the Theologian, was appointed Bishop of Constantinople in AD 379. He contended with the Arians, defending the Comma. In opposing them, he had set forth the above argument. In his Fifth Theological Orations on the Holy Spirit, he said as follows:

> What about John then, when in his Catholic Epistle he says that there are three that bear witness, the Spirit and the Water, and the Blood? Do you think he is talking nonsense? First, because he ventures to reckon, under one numeral, things which are not consubstantial,

---

[49] Special thanks to Larry Bridgen, Senior Editor Consultant of the Trinitarian Bible Society for this additional insight on the passage.

though you say this ought to be done only in the case of things which are consubstantial. For who would assert that these are consubstantial? Secondly, because he had not been consistent in the way he has happened upon his terms; for after using three in the masculine gender he added three words which are neuter, contrary to the definitions and laws which you and your grammarians have laid down. For what is the difference between putting the masculine three first, and then adding one and one and one in the neuter, or after a masculine? One and one and one to use the three not in the masculine but in the neuter, which you yourself disclaim in the case of Deity.[50]

As one can readily see, Gregory's argument stems from the basic principles of Greek grammar. He is simply saying that one cannot mix the neuter with the masculine. He used terms such as "consubstantial" and "non–consubstantial," pointing out that there is an unnatural mixture of the nature of things if the Trinitarian passage were omitted. Therefore, he was insistent upon the acceptance of the Trinitarian Witness on the grounds of the fundamental rules of grammar. The testimony of the three witnesses, he argued, cannot be rejected, because the grammatical construction demands it. Otherwise, what is said is reduced to utter nonsense!

Neither should we entertain the thought that the eighth verse is an ellipsis, as Facundus suggests.[51] That is, the

---

50 Gregory of Nazianzus, *The Post Nicene and Post Nicene Fathers* (Grand Rapids, MI: Erdmann Publishing Company, 1978), 233-234.

51 (Scrivener, A Plain introduction to the New Testament Textual Criticism 405)

In Defense of the Authenticity of 1 John 5:7

Trinitarian witness is to be understood because of the very construction of verse eight. When one says that verse eight is an ellipsis, all he is doing is seeking to justify the removal of the Comma and at the same time seeking to compensate for the abnormality of the grammatical construction. That is why it is argued that verse eight is an ellipsis. It is far more reasonable to accept *"the Father, the Word, and the Holy Ghost"* as supplied in verse seven than to say that *"the Father, the Word, and the Holy Ghost"* are implied. Even Dr. Scrivener, as we earlier read, is cited against Facundus.

The reader should also consider the date when Gregory of Nazianzus set forth this dissertation demanding the acceptance of the Comma. It was in AD 379. It was then that the Arians had control over the Greek Church. At that time, the Arians were beginning to be challenged. Soon their hold on the church would be broken. They were never able to get the Greek Orthodox Church to accept their heretical doctrine denying the deity of our Lord. It was in the heat of this battle that Gregory was demanding the acceptance of the Comma based upon the grammatical rules of the Greek language, which they apparently ignored in copying the manuscripts.

This argument set forth by Gregory of Nazianzus is quite revealing, not only in regard to the grammatical argument that he had so well set forth in the defense of the Comma, but also from his treatise. There are two other things that should be observed. The first is that the Comma was attested to as early as, if not earlier than, AD 379 in the Greek manuscripts! If it were not, then Gregory would not have argued for it. Thus it is a well–established fact that the disputed passage was in copies of the Greek manuscripts as early as, if not earlier than, AD 379. Also, the debate over the Comma was argued and settled in the Greek Church before

Jerome's Vulgate of AD 385. This timing is interesting since Jerome, contemporary with Gregory, omitted the Comma.

As was stated earlier, the Arians took over the Greek Church, shortly after Constantine came into power, and mutilated the Scriptures. This is apparent in that they were seeking to remove the Comma from the sacred text for which Gregory so strongly contended. If this were not the case, why then was this contention over the Comma between Gregory and the Arians? Those who were at the helm of the Greek Church at that time were guilty of omitting the Comma to fit their theology. It was not uncommon in those days for men to corrupt the Scriptures to fit their theology. Also, they used corrupt copies of the Scriptures that omitted the Comma as those produced in the Alexandrian school.

It is important to keep in mind that while Gregory in the Greek Church was contending for the Comma and restored it to its proper place, Jerome a few years later used corrupt manuscripts of Eusebius in producing the Latin Vulgate and thus omitted the Comma from the Holy Scriptures. Jerome was inclined to lean upon Eusebius, the semi–Arian, than upon the great Greek theologian, Gregory of Nazianzus. However, Jerome's Vulgate as produced was never accepted.

Then, almost fifteen hundred years later, Gregory's argument again resurfaced. But this time, it was not against the modern–day Arians but rather against the School of Higher Textual Criticism. These critics looked upon the Comma with a jaundiced eye and sought to remove it from the English Bible, placing it in brackets. In time, they had accomplished their end, eliminating the Comma altogether from the modern translations.

It was the great R. L. Dabney, one of the greatest thinkers and scholars since Jonathan Edwards, who rose up to meet the challenge. He wrote:

The internal evidence against the excision, then is in the following strong points; First if it be made, the masculine, article, numeral, and participle, οι τρεις μαρτυρουντες, are made to agree directly with the three neuters— an insuperable and very bald grammatical difficulty. But if the disputed words are allowed to stand, they agree directly with the two masculiness and one neuter nouns, ο πατηρ, ο λογος, και το αγιον πνευ–μα

where, according to a well known rule of syntax, the masculine among the group control the gender over the neuter connected with them.

Then the occurrence of the masculine τρεις μαρτυρουντες in the eighth verse agreeing with the neuters, πνευμα υδωρ and αιμα may be accounted for by the power of attraction, so well known in Greek syntax, and by the fact that the πνευμα, the leading noun of this second group, and next to the adjectives, has just had a species of the masculineness super induced upon it by its previous position in the masculine group.[52]

R. L. Dabney, by reasoning and logically working through the difficulty, arrived at the same conclusion as that of Gregory and others after him. In spite of what the so–called scholars affirm concerning the lack of witnesses in the Greek manuscripts, Dabney was compelled to accept the authenticity of the Comma simply upon the grammatical construction of the text.

---

52 Robert L. Dabney, *Discussions*, (Carlisle, PA: The Banner of Truth Trust, 1982), Vol. I, 377-378.

The writer does not wish to imply that these were the only scholars who argued for the acceptance of the Comma from the internal evidence. There were many other scholars who demanded its acceptance upon the same grounds such as Fredrick Nolan, whom Dabney cites, and Edward Hills. There was also Archdeacon Travis in 1790, the pride of Cambridge, who is said to have set forth a strong defense for the acceptance of the Johanneum Comma based upon the internal witness. After him, there was Charles Froster whose work entitled "A New Plea for the Authenticity of the Text of the Three Heavenly Witnesses" was published in 1857. This is said to be one of the best works published on this subject. It would be good to revive these works so that the present generation might have access to them. However, it seems that they are buried and hidden from the public's eyes. (As one can readily see, the leaven of corruption was already at work. It was at work prior to the gathering of the revision committee in 1870.)

Neither should the reader overlook other scholars, such as Erasmus, Beza, Stephens, and the Elsevier brothers. All these men produced their edition of the Greek New Testament, and all, without exception, never questioned the authenticity of the Comma. All of their editions of the Greek New Testament contained the Comma as it is presently set forth in the received text. There was not the slightest variation among them on this passage. The various editions of the Greek New Testament that were produced over a period of more than a century were all in agreement. None even questioned the authenticity of this passage that is presently questioned by modern scholars.

All the above critics had a few differences in their editions of the New Testament, but as to their differences, there were only thirty–three, and these are so insignificant, they are not even worth mentioning. However, for those who

In Defense of the Authenticity of 1 John 5:7

swallow camels and strain at gnats, this might be another matter. The writer has examined each of these variations and has shown them in a former work to be so insignificant that they are not worth mentioning. In the future, the writer may publish this work if there is a demand for it. However, many of these variations were merely a matter of spelling. The only reason these variations were ever catalogued was to promote the Critical Text.

All men, if not prejudiced, should arrive without hesitation at the same conclusion as that of R. L. Dabney and others when viewing the internal evidence. The Comma must be retained. It is foolish to assume because men pass themselves off as scholars that they know everything and are not to be questioned! Surely the reader by this time should realize that the simple, elementary rules of Greek grammar demand the acceptance of this disputed passage. This is the only conclusion to which one can safely arrive if one reasons without prejudices.

Hence in light of the internal witness, the Comma must without dispute stand. We know that both the Ante—Nicene and Post–Nicene Fathers quoted it. We also know that it is attested to in the Greek manuscripts though not as pronounced as we would like. But it is still there even though the Scriptures were attacked from without as well as from within the Greek Church. It is overwhelmingly attested to in the Old Latin and in the Latin Vulgate. This is not to mention other translations of the Scriptures, lexicons, and the church fathers who also quoted the disputed passage. In fact, it is universally found throughout the church regardless of whether the saints were in Africa, Europe, or Asia Minor.

Furthermore, it has been in the English Bible for five centuries, and it was never questioned until of late. Therefore, we must never think that the Johanneum Comma entered into the Scriptures through some pious scribe, as not a few speculate. Rather, we ought to conclude from the preponderance of evidences that the Comma is an authentic portion of the Holy Scriptures which our Lord has preserved to all generations. And as for the internal evidences, the case is shut. The argument is conclusive. There is no voice that can be raised against it. The Comma must stand because basic Greek grammar demands it. This witness is irrefutable!

(the Biblical passages italicized were for emphasis only)

> For ever settled in the Heav'ns
> Thy Word, O Lord, shall firmly stand;
> Thy faithfulness shall never fail;
> The earth abides at Thy Command.
>
> Thy Word and works unmoved remain,
> Thine ev'ry Purpose to fulfill;
> All things are thine and Thee obey,
> And all as servants wait Thy Will.
>
> I should have perished in my woe
> Had not I loved thy law divine;
> That law I never can forget;
> And all as servants wait thy will.
>
> The wicked would destroy my soul,
> But in thy truth is refuge sure;
> Exceeding broad is Thy command,
> And in perfection shall endure.

–Psalm 119: 89–97, the Psalter, 1912

Chapter 5

Further Discussion of the Internal Witness

There will always be those who will insist on omitting the Trinitarian passage regardless of the evidences that are set forth. Their minds are made up. Therefore, to them there is nothing to be said. What is presently written is not to convince them of their error but to strengthen the saints. There is a need not only of exposing the erroneous arguments that are presented in opposition to the Comma but of revealing further internal evidences that demand inclusion of 1 John 5:7.

For example, it is argued that the reason the masculine adjectives and participle are used in verse eight, (και τρεις εστιν οι μαρτυρvντες εν τη γη) "...there are three that bear witness in earth...", is because "the Spirit" is a person. Therefore, the masculine must be used. The Holy Spirit no doubt is a person. This is undeniable. However, the apostle in referring to the Holy Spirit in the sixth verse of this very chapter does not use the masculine article and participle in referring to Him. Instead, he uses the neuter article and participle as he wrote (και το πνευμα εστι το μερτυρουν) "And it is the Spirit that beareth witness..." This is because the word "Spirit" in the Greek is neuter. The use of the neuter in no way denies that the Holy Spirit is a person. Therefore, such an argument has no foundation. It should never even be entertained.

Others seek to discredit the Trinitarian passage by pointing out that there are other grammatical abnormalities in Scripture and this is just another one of them. In seeking to fluff off the obvious, they are ready to dismiss the grammatical principles of the language rather than seek to understand the reason for these "apparent" abnormalities. Citing other difficulties never resolves the problem but rather glosses over it. It is a cheap ploy used to hold onto their ill–founded position while seeking to confuse their opponent. It is amazing what lengths people go to in order to reject truth. As for these so–called abnormalities, once they are carefully examined, it will be realized that they do not violate the principles of Greek grammar at all.

Critics argue that so few Greek manuscripts contain the Comma. However, the Comma has been quoted by the church fathers throughout the centuries. There is a great host of witnesses that testify to it. Many of them testify to the Comma long before the earliest manuscripts we presently have in our possession. Some of these church fathers are mentioned in the appendix. Critics, however, ignore these witnesses, claiming that they are of little or no value. The number of manuscripts and the dating of them are purportedly of more importance. I ask, is one honest who dismisses these witnesses of the church?

To ignore the witness of the church fathers is alarming. Why are such witnesses claimed to be irrelevant? We are told to consider only the manuscripts themselves. Whoever came up with such a principle as that? And why are we compelled to accept it? Have we not read, "…the church of the living God, the pillar and ground of the truth" 1 Timothy 3:15? The church is the guardian of the truth, not the world. And the church universally throughout the ages has testified to the Comma. What shall we make of that?

Opponents to the Comma ignore how the Roman Empire and the Arians destroyed the Scriptures. Neither do we know how many copies of the Scriptures were destroyed by wars, fires and calamities. (These things were earlier mentioned.) But what we do know is that God has preserved His Word. To just count manuscripts and then make a decision based upon their number is ludicrous. How can any sober—minded person ever entertain such an outlandish principle as that?

Consider how in the days of King Josiah it appears that there was but one single copy of the Law which was rediscovered in the shambles of the temple. Shall we question the Books of Moses because there were so few copies at that time? Nonsense!! The fact that there were so few copies of the Scriptures that existed after godless hands sought to destroy and amend them only testifies to the faithfulness of God in preserving His Word. Out of the ashes of destroyed empires and civilizations and the multitude of martyrs the Word of God abideth still! This is a wonder. It is a marvel! God has faithfully preserved His Word as He had promised (Matthew 24:35).

On the positive side, the principle of attraction is a well–known rule of Greek grammar. It demands the inclusion of the Comma when reading 1 John 5:8, which was earlier discussed. However, it would be good to again pause and reflect upon this very passage. Further evidence demands the inclusion of the Comma. Consider the words following the neuter substantives, "the Spirit, and the water, and the blood," και οι τριες εις το εν εισιν, "…and these three agree in one." All these words are masculine except (το εν) which is literally "the one" which is neuter. The grammatical structure of this eighth verse is very interesting as it moves from masculine to neuter, and then back to masculine, and finally back to neuter. Surely this should arrest the reader.

First, we have the masculine, "and there are three that bear witness in earth" followed by the three neuter substantives, "the Spirit, and the water, and the blood." Immediately following these neuter nouns we read και οι τριες "and these three" which is masculine. There is no doubt that these words "these three things" refer to "the Spirit, and the water, and the blood" which are all neuter. How is this explained? The words "and these three" do not directly refer back to the three neuter substantives. They refer back to the three witnesses on the earth in the beginning of the eighth verse which are masculine. This grammatical structure conclusively serves to reinforce the argument in favor of the Comma.

Accordingly, this principle of syntax explains the other passages that are thrown at those who defend the Comma. It is said that there are other abnormalities in the Scriptures such as 1 Corinthians 13:13. Although faith, hope and love are feminine, they are referred to in neuter, τα τρια τυατα, "these three things." The Apostle is addressing spiritual gifts and especially those spiritual gifts that the saints should covet. Therefore faith, hope and love are referred to in the neuter because they are spiritual gifts. No abnormalities exist if one applies a simple understanding of the rules of syntax.

But one does not have to know Greek to understand the necessity of the inclusion of the Comma. The preposition in verse eight demands its inclusion, or the reader would be left dangling when reading "and these three agree in [the] one." R. L. Dabney rightly asks, who is "the one" in which "the spirit, and the water, and the blood" agree? If it is not "the one" of the seventh verse, then what are we to make of what is said?[53]

It is arresting that in the Greek we have the definite article which is often omitted in translating over into English. With its inclusion, the reading becomes even more pronounced as we read "and these three agree in [the] one." Again, who then is *the* one in which they agree? "The one" has to be, as R. L. Dabney stated, the foresaid "one" in verse seven. As anyone can readily see, there is no other "one" mentioned other than *the* one in 1 John 5:7.

However, in light of what is said, there are still those who insist in omitting the Comma. For example, M. R. Vincent in his Greek word studies rejects the Comma as he followed the position of the higher critics. As to his explanation of the preposition he says that *the* one of 1 John 5:8 refers to or converges upon Christ.[54] Thus the three witnesses of verse eight "agree in one" who is Christ. This is a popular position that men have taken who reject the Comma. Even in some of the newer translations such as the ESV, it substitutes *the* one with "Christ."

But the grammatical principle of Greek will not allow such an interpretation. This is because the words (το εν) in the eighth verse, "the one" are neuter. If *the* one in the preposition of the eighth verse referred to Christ Jesus, the Messiah, the Son of God or the Son of man, then it would have to be masculine as all of these titles of our Lord are masculine. Hence such an interpretation of this passage cannot stand. The neuter prohibits it.

---

53 (Dabney 377-378)
54 Marvin R. Vincent, *Word Studies in the New Testament* (Wilmington, DE: Associated Publishers, 1972), 545.

The question with which we are faced is how are we to explain the neuter in the preposition of verse eight, "agree in one"? The only explanation is that it must refer back to *the* one of verse seven which is also neuter. It is as R. L. Dabney has so perceptively stated. In this majestic passage, "the Father, the Word, and the Holy Ghost: and these three are one", we are told that they are not only One but they are also of One substance and essence. This is because God is a spirit. This is what John tells us in John 4:24. "Spirit" as we have previously gathered is neuter. Thus the neuter "are one" which is used in verse seven, "εν εισι," is arresting when following the masculine, "the Father, the Word, and the Holy Ghost." (Spirit by association with the Father and Son becomes masculine) How precise the apostle is in his writing!

Then in the eighth verse we read, "and these three agree in one", "και οι τρεις εις το εν εισιν." In both passages, "one" is neuter! This too should arrest the reader. The One in which the witnesses on the earth agree is the same One of the seventh verse which is God! If we allow the Comma to stand, then all confusion is dismissed. Otherwise, we would be left in a state of confusion, and in seeking to overcome it, we would corrupt the Scriptures.

Also, when reflecting upon the gospel of John, the reader will discover that this is not something new with the apostle. For an example in John 10:30 our Lord made a tremendous claim. He said, "I and my Father are one." The Jews understood His claim and took up stones to stone Him. Although the Father and our Lord are masculine, yet our Lord used the neuter numeral one ("εν") to refer to them as being one. Hence the claim of our Lord was not that He and the Father were one in agreement as Arians argue, but one in substance and essence. How consistent John is in his writings! When one examines 1 John 5:8, it is readily seen that it cannot stand apart from the Comma. The preposition of 1 John 5:8 will not allow it.

Furthermore, what must be considered is what the apostle is seeking to establish. There are two irrefutable witnesses to the person of our Lord Jesus Christ. There is not only the witness in heaven, "the Father, the Word, and the Holy Ghost" that testify to the person of our Lord, but there is also the witness on earth as well, "the spirit, and the water, and the blood." Furthermore, the witness on earth agrees in *the* one which is the testimony of the Holy Trinity. What John establishes is that there are two witnesses who agree in their testimony to the person of our Lord. The one witness is from Heaven and the other is on the earth. Furthermore, these two witnesses agree in their testimony.

One cannot read the gospel of John and fail to see how the apostle is keenly conscious of the necessity of the two witnesses agreeing in their testimony. All one has to do is read John chapter five and John chapter eight to sense this very line of thought running through his gospel. The testimony of one witness alone is not sufficient. Therefore, there must be two or more witnesses who agree in order to establish a credible witness. Hence,1 John 5:7–8 presents the witnesses on earth agreeing in the credibility of the testimony of Jesus the Christ, the Son of God, the Savior of the world. This is a very important point which the apostle sets forth.....and it must not be overlooked!

Consider how this principle of two witnesses is required by our God. This law is mentioned twice in Deuteronomy and practiced throughout the Scriptures. Even in the trial of our Lord, the Sanhedrin labored to find two witnesses who agreed so that they could condemn our Lord to death but found none. They were acting according to the law as stated in Deuteronomy 17:6 "At the mouth of two witnesses, or three witnesses, shall he that is worthy of death be put to death; but at the mouth of one witness he shall not be put to death." And again in Deuteronomy 19:15 it is stated, "One witness shall not rise up against a man for any iniquity, or for any sin, in any sin that he sinneth: at the mouth of two witnesses, or at the mouth of three witnesses, shall the matter be established."

Therefore to remove the Trinitarian passage would drastically weaken the testimony to the person of our Lord and Savior, Jesus Christ. We would be left with the single witnesses on earth; and the final preposition "agree in (the) one" would make no sense. Who or what is (the) "one" to which it is said they agree? Keep in mind that the witnesses must agree. But if we let verse seven stand, then the witnesses on the earth would be in agreement with "the" one" of verse seven, the Father, the Word and the Spirit. Thus at the mouth of two or more witnesses in agreement, the matter stands.

Why is this so important? It is stated in the words of 1 John 5:13, "These things have I written unto you that believe on the name of the Son of God; that ye may know that ye have eternal life, and that ye may believe on the name of the Son of God."

Thy Word is like a garden, Lord

Thy word is like a garden, Lord
With flower bright and fair;
And ev'ry one who seeks, may pluck
A lovely cluster there.

Thy Word is a deep, deep mine,
And Jewels rich and rare
Are hidden in its mighty depths
For ev'ry searcher there.

In Defense of the Authenticity of 1 John 5:7

Oh may I love Thy precious Word,
May I explore the mine
May I its fragrant flowers glean,
May light upon me shine!

Oh, may I find my armor there!
Thy Word my trusty sword,
I'll learn to fight with ev'ry foe,
The battle of the Lord.

by Edwin Hodder

CHAPTER 6

Reflections

It is only fair to acknowledge that there are many who reject the Comma. Many of these men are Naturalists and Unitarians. These men do not believe in the deity of our Lord Jesus Christ and are no different in many respects than the Arians of the fourth century. However, in other respects, they may differ in that they altogether deny the supernatural. At least the Arians of the fourth century believed in the supernatural but denied the deity of our Lord Christ Jesus. However, they all have one thing in common; they reject the Comma. If they would ever come to accept the Comma, then they would have to correct their theology concerning the deity of our Lord Jesus Christ.

But then there are others who have simply been led astray by the so–called pseudo–scholars. This includes many professing Christians. They too have come to deny the authenticity of 1 John 5:7. Dr. F. H. Scrivener, an esteemed scholar and textual critic, looked upon the Comma as being spurious. In his writings on textual criticism, at times he showed himself to be a contradiction of parts. He stated the only value of the Vaticanus and Sinaiticus was their antiquity. But later he changed his opinion on these two corrupt manuscripts and considered them as valuable witnesses. In regard to the Comma he wrote:

> We have said before that it is perfectly gratuitous to allege fraud against those who introduced the Three Heavenly Witnesses by way of spiritual comment, first into the margin of this Epistle, then into the text. That it has no right to hold a place in the body of Scripture we regard as certain. It belongs not to the whole Christian church, but to a single branch of it, and in early times to one fruitful offshoot of that branch.[55]

Many sincere saints have rejected the Comma because of this very supposition. They have come to assume the position of Dr. Scrivener. It is supposed that the Comma was first placed in the margin of the text and later made its way into the text itself. This has been stated so often that it is presently accepted as fact. We who believe in the preservation of the Holy Scriptures are always put to the task of answering a barrage of unceasing questions. At this time, the writer would like to propose a few.

Is it proper to admit as evidence or to be taken as a fact something that is assumed when there are no proofs to support such assumptions? Is it not an assumption that the Comma was first placed in the margin and later made its way into the Scriptures? Surely we must not accept assumptions and so–called "conjectural emendations" as facts. Would it not be far more reasonable to consider that the copyist placed the Comma in the margin because he accidently omitted it when copying the manuscript rather than to

---

55 (Scrivener, Six Lectures on the Text of the New Testament 206)

assume that some unknown scribe placed the Comma in the margin and later it was incorporated into the text?

Keep in mind that the eye of the copyists could easily have fallen from verse seven to verse eight while copying Scripture. This would explain why verse seven was so widely omitted. One passage that is notoriously omitted because of such carelessness is John 3:16. This is because John 3:15 is much like John 3:16. In like manner, 1 John 5:7 is very similar to 1 John 5:8.

Now consider for a moment how a scribe could have unintentionally omitted the Comma in copying the Scriptures. The reader should take into consideration how similar these two passages are. Both of these passages read identically the same in the beginning. Both of these verses read, "τρεις εστι οι μαρτυρουντες εν" (Literally translated, "three are the witnesses in"). Also keep in mind that there were no spaces between the words as there are above. All the letters ran together. This made copying Scriptures even more difficult.

Then consider how the copyist's eye in copying the Scriptures was constantly moving from the parchment he was copying to the parchment upon which he was writing. Try to visualize after copying the words, τρειςεστινοιμαρτυρουντεςεν of verse seven, he then looked up, and instead of his eyes falling upon the seventh verse, it now falls upon the eighth verse, which reads exactly the same at this point. In reading the words he just copied, τρειςεστινοιμαρτυρουντεςεν, and instead of finishing copying the latter part of the seventh verse, he commences to copy the latter part of verse eight.

One can readily understand how the copyist, due to human weaknesses and common frailties, unintentionally omitted the rest of the seventh verse, "The Father, the Word, and the Holy Ghost," and instead copied the remainder of the eighth verse, "the spirit, and the water, and the blood." As anyone can see, there are very few differences between these two passages. Also, it is quite understandable how easily this could have happened when we consider the constant movement of the copyist's eye from parchment to parchment. It is far more reasonable to assume a copyist's error in inadvertently omitting the Three Witnesses than a copyist taking it upon himself to blatantly add the Comma in the margin of the Sacred Text.

When considering the tedious task of copying the Holy Oracles, one must remember that errors of this nature were quite common in copying manuscripts. Sometimes scribes would accidently copy the same passage twice. Sometimes they would omit an entire passage altogether. Such errors exist in copies of the manuscripts that we presently have in our possession. Thus, the omission of the Trinitarian passage no doubt was an oversight rather than an interpolation.

The reader should not be troubled that such blunders exist in the copies of the Scriptures we have in our possession. We have so many manuscripts in our possession that such errors can easily be detected and corrected. These human errors do not pose a problem. At one time, it was the task of the true textual critics to edit the manuscripts, filtering out such errors. However, today, the modern textual critics have taken it upon themselves to determine what is and what is not Scripture. There is a world of difference between the two schools of textual criticism. The former critics of the school of textual criticism were editors. As for the latter, they are composers. This explains why at one time we had the same Bible in the English tongue for four hundred years, and presently, we have a proliferation of translations of the English Bible, all differing from each other.

The point, however, is this: would it not be far more reasonable to assume that the Comma was inadvertently omitted, and in rereading the manuscript, the scribe then placed the Comma in the margin, correcting the mistake rather than recopying the entire leaf? And would not the copyist following him copy the Scriptures as they were given to him or even make the same error? The textual critics of the School of Higher Textual Criticism hold the copyists in very low esteem. They assume that copyists would take it upon themselves to embellish the Scriptures as they pleased. Therefore, these revisionists took it upon themselves as their responsibility to correct these so–called embellishments made by the scribes. They had no intention of editing the manuscripts before them but rather to recreate a Bible the church never knew.

But on the other hand, suppose that the Comma was added to the Scriptures. Should we not inquire what scribe or scribes dared to place the Comma in the Scriptures? At what time did the Comma first make its way into the Text? Who was that person who dared commit such a dastardly deed as this? If a scribe added the Comma to the Sacred Scriptures, how is it that there was no outcry against it until some eighteen hundred years later! Are these not reasonable questions?

Furthermore, how does Dr. Scrivener's argument stand in light of the earliest extant copy of 1 John that is dated tenth century? If the earliest manuscript 221 (as introduced in chapter 1) had the disputed passage in the margin, is it suggested that from thence the Comma began to make its way into the Scriptures? This is not acceptable, for we know that the disputed text was in the Greek manuscripts as far back as AD 379. Gregory of Nazianzus disputed with the Arians concerning the Comma at that time. The Arians were omitting the Comma, and Gregory, in turn, was demanding its inclusion. How then does this line up with Dr. Scrivener's argument?

In Defense of the Authenticity of 1 John 5:7

How did the Comma that was supposedly first placed in the margin in the tenth century (AD 900-1000) make its way into the Sacred Scriptures when it was in the Greek manuscripts as far back as AD 379? If it was added, as Dr. Scrivener supposes, then the Comma had to be added sometime before the tenth century or even sometime before AD 379. If the Comma was added at that time, it was not in the margin, but rather, it had to be in the text. This is apparent since Gregory argued for its authenticity from syntax. He defended its presence, not protesting against its absence. To those who affirm that the Comma was first placed in the margin and later made its way into the text we ask, "When was that?" The answer given is, "We do not know!" So much for facts!

Also, are we to presume one man added the Comma into the Sacred Scriptures and others, without question, copied something that was foreign to the Scriptures? This would be highly questionable, since the church separated the heretical writings from the authentic. It is unconscionable to suggest that scribes dared add anything to the Scriptures. The scribes' task was to copy the Scriptures as they were set before them, and that was all they were to do. And that was all that they did. It is absurd to imply that they would add or take away from the Scriptures. Such charges are more than ludicrous; they are criminal. Unless evidence can be brought forth to incriminate these scribes, then such charges must be silenced. We have literally thousands of manuscripts, and we do not have any scribe throughout the centuries embellishing the Scriptures. This is with the exception of heretics. Therefore, such assumptions as those of the School of Higher Textual Criticism should never be entertained.

Furthermore, if someone had added the Comma to the Scriptures, as not a few assert, why was it not challenged? Surely the church would have challenged a crime of this magnitude. Could anyone have dared to add anything to the Word of God and not be challenged by the church? Are we to assume that those early saints were not jealous guardians of the Sacred Oracles? What would warrant such thoughts? We have earlier established that historically, Christians were people of the Book. They laid down their lives unto death before they would turn the Holy Writings over to unholy hands to be destroyed. Surely, there would have been a cry of outrage if anything were added to the Sacred Oracles. But we have no record of anything of this nature ever taking place. The adding of the Comma to the Sacred Text is an invention of this new breed of critics.

Also, if the Old Latin text was translated from the Greek, and without question it was, then we are compelled to inquire, how did the Comma enter into the Old Latin text if it were not in the Greek text? The writer does not recall anyone answering that question. All that is said is that the Comma was only in one branch of the church. Well, how did it get there? For that matter, how did it get into the Syrian Peshitto or into the Waldenses' French and Italian Bibles? Better still, how did it get into our English translations? Are we to assume that men carelessly or irreverently translated the Holy Word of God? This is what the School of Higher Textual Criticism would have us believe. The writer will not accept that! The godly always handled the Scriptures with reverence, and God superintends the transmission of the Scriptures to all generations.

And as for the Comma being found in only one branch of the church, this argument is questioned by scholars.[56] As was pointed out earlier, the Old Latin manuscripts that were discovered were found in Italy, not Africa. And as it was earlier observed, all of the Old Latin manuscripts of 1 John

---

56 (Scrivener, A Plain introduction to the New Testament Textual Criticism 43-44)

In Defense of the Authenticity of 1 John 5:7

have the Comma. So much for Dr. Scrivener's judgment that the Comma was limited to only one branch of the church.

It is interesting that when Erasmus omitted 1 John 5:7 in his first two editions of the Greek New Testament, there was a great outcry of protest from the church at large. Many today imply that Erasmus placed the Comma in the latter three editions because of the pressure of the people for him to do so. The people were outraged because of its omission and rightly so because he was taking away from the Sacred Scriptures. This is only mentioned to show how widely the Comma was accepted.

Later when Erasmus discovered the Comma in a Greek manuscript, and realizing that it was so pronounced in the Latin, he was compelled not only because of the outcry of the people but also by his own conscience to restore the Comma in his later three editions of his Greek New Testament. When he restored the Comma in its proper place, he was challenged only by a few for doing so. Again, by his own confession, he argued that the text had to be in the Greek Scriptures because it was in the Latin.[57] Interesting deduction!

On the other hand, when Jerome omitted the Comma in his translation of the Latin Vulgate in AD 384–385, there was a great cry of outrage throughout the Latin Church. Jerome was accused of corrupting the Bible in using corrupt manuscripts to produce the Latin Vulgate. The reader should find this interesting. When the Comma was omitted, there is a record of the time and the place and even of the persons who sought to omit it. This is not only true with Jerome but also with Erasmus and the Arians before them as well. But when it comes to the addition of the Comma into the Scriptures, as some suppose, there is an absolute dead

---

57 (Erasmus 137)

silence as to the time, place and person that did it. The argument given is, "Probably some unknown scribe placed the Comma in the margin and in time it made its way into the Bible itself."[58] Isn't this a pitiful argument for removing a passage from the Scriptures. This is especially so when the Comma was universally accepted for almost two millennia.

If the Comma were an addition to the Scriptures that took place in the African church, are we to believe that Sabellius and his followers would not have vehemently challenged it?[59] Surely there would have been an outcry because he and his followers believed that the one God was manifested in three different ways. They denied the three persons of the Godhead. He, as his followers, openly opposed the Trinitarian doctrine. We have no record of anyone challenging the three witnesses; instead, we have record of Sabellius repenting of his position and embracing the doctrine of the Trinity.

If the Comma were added to the Scriptures by the Greek Church, would there not have been an outcry by the Arians who violently opposed the doctrine of the Trinity? But again, we have no record of anything of that nature taking place. Nowhere is there to be found, throughout the annals of Christian history, a voice protesting the Trinitarian passage being added to the Sacred Scriptures by the Arians. Instead there is a strange silence on their part. Modern scholars assume that the Comma had been added. Assumptions are never to be accepted as facts. Never!

However, we have the record of the controversy in the Greek Church as early as AD 379 with the Arians seeking to remove the Comma. But when it comes to adding the Comma to the Scriptures, there is a dead silence. The Arians were not challenging Gregory for adding the Comma, but

---

58 (Scrivener, Six Lectures on the Text of the New Testament 206)
59 (Sabellius), Bishop of the African Church that denied the Trinity

rather, Gregory challenged the Arians for omitting the Comma from the Sacred Text. This in itself is telling.

Furthermore, the reading of 1 John 5:6–8 with the omission of the seventh verse makes the reading very awkward. It is not only awkward, but it is also confusing. The reading makes no sense. How much smoother the reading of the text becomes when the seventh verse is allowed to stand. It also removes the confusion from what is being said. Thus the reading with the inclusion of the seventh verse makes the reading clear and comprehensive and not disconnected and confusing.

The School of Higher Textual Criticism had set forth new laws that, up to that time, were unknown. They were canons of their making. One of their canons states that the rougher reading is to be preferred over the smooth reading. If the disputed passage makes the reading smooth, then on this ground alone it is to be rejected and the rough reading is to be preferred. So if a copy of the Scriptures had the Comma omitted and another had the passage retained, the rough reading would be accepted over the smooth reading. When did absurdity become acceptable? And upon what ground was this foolish axiom made?

Westcott and Hort suggest why such absurdities are to be accepted. They wrote in their book, *Introduction to the New Testament in the Original Greek,* that the disposition of the scribe would be to "smooth away difficulties; which were the foundation of a paradoxical precept to 'choose the harder reading, the most famous of all canons of criticism.'"[60] "The most famous of all canons of criticism"; watch out for these sophistries!

Now what is the reasoning behind this canon? How is it that modern textual critics would ever entertain such an

---

60 (Brooke F. Westcott and Fenton J. A. Hort 28)

absurdity? They assume that the copyists would add to the Scriptures in order "to smooth away difficulties" and make the rough readings smoother. Notice this is not stated as a supposition but as a fact. They did not write, "They would most likely," but rather, "They would"! This is another example of the liberties these unscrupulous men took upon themselves to corrupt the Scriptures.

The question we must face is, are we, upon such an assumption, to expunge the Comma from the Sacred Oracles? How is it that we fail to believe the copyists handled the Sacred Scriptures with great reverence? How can anyone accept that they would take upon themselves to add to or take away from the Holy Word of God? Remember, these saints forfeited their lives rather than give up the Holy Scriptures to be burned. The light of the testimony of these saints shines as beacons to this day. Are we to think that they would handle the Sacred Word of God as a piece of profane literature? God forbid! Banish such nonsense!

These modern textual critics also set up another law; the shorter readings were to be preferred to the longer readings, assuming that scribes would have a tendency to embellish or add to the Scriptures. It is apparent that these critics have absolutely no reverence for the Sacred Scriptures. They fail to acknowledge the holy hand of Providence preserving the Holy Oracles. If God sustains every seed–bearing tree and plant on this earth, shall He not much more preserve the incorruptible seed *"…the word of God, which liveth and abideth forever" (1 Peter 1:23)?*

Why would anyone ever entertain such rules as these? Common sense demands the opposite. If something does not read understandably, immediately the rational mind realizes that there is something wrong! Yet intelligent men, who have put together the Critical Greek Text, made up absurd rules and fixed them as the unalterable law as that

In Defense of the Authenticity of 1 John 5:7

of the Medes and Persians. But what is worse still is that these critics ask the saints to take leave of their senses and rest solely upon *their* authority. We have gone back to Rome!

Therefore there is no reason to accept the absurd rule that some pious scribe inserted the Comma into the margin, which later made its way into the Bible. Neither should one assume that the copyists embellished or added to the Holy Oracles in order to make the rough readings smoother. Such thoughts should never be entertained until some kind of proof is brought forth to support such claims. Yet there are many who have assumed such innuendoes to be facts. May God help us!

If these critics are to challenge the Comma, then the burden of proof rests upon them. They must prove their accusations with facts, which they do not have. Assumptions are not acceptable. To what extremes we may soar when we do not have our feet planted firmly on the ground and our heads are in the clouds! The burden of proof for the validity of the Comma does not rest upon those who accept the Trinitarian passage because the evidences for the Comma are indisputable. But let them commence by refuting the evidences that testify on its behalf.

In the final analysis, we must inquire why the Greek Orthodox Church to this day has no problem with the Comma. They do not even question it. Presently, it stands indisputably in the Greek Bible. Are we to suppose that they are ignorant? Are we to assume that they have no scholars? Such notions are ludicrous. What shall we say of Gregory of Nazianzus, the Theologian? What a champion of truth he was. He was a David who withstood Goliath and was victorious!

And what shall we say of Cyril Lucaris I, the brilliant statesman and scholar? He was the esteemed patriarch of the seventeenth century who stands out as a radiant star in a dark day. His radiance yet shines unto this day as one of the greatest minds and textual critics of all time. It was he who gave the Greeks their Bible in their modern tongue. And as a foremost scholar, he never for a moment questioned the Comma. Should not these facts provoke the minds of those who reject it?

One would think that if the Comma did not belong in the Greek Bible, the Greek Orthodox Church would be the first to challenge it. They of all people would know. After all, was not the Greek Orthodox Church for centuries the sole guardian of the Greek manuscripts? If any people would have known that the Comma was spurious, surely they would be the ones to know. But to the surprise of many, they not only accept the Comma, but they also furiously defend it. The subject is not even open for debate. We would do well to follow their example!

> The Bible stands like a rock un–daunted
> 'Mid the raging storms of time;
> Its pages burn with the truth eternal,
> And they glow with a light sublime.
>
> The Bible stands as a mountain tow'ring
> Far above the works of men;
> Its truth by none ever was refuted,
> And destroy it they never can.
>
> The Bible stands and it will forever
> When the world has passed away;
> By inspiration it has been given,
> All its precepts I will obey.

In Defense of the Authenticity of 1 John 5:7

The Bible stands ev'ry test we give it,
For its Author is divine;
By grace alone I expect to live it,
And to prove it and make it mine.

The Bible stands tho' the hills may tumble,
It will firmly stand when the earth shall crumble;
I will plant my feet on its firm foundation,
For the Bible stands. Amen!

–Haldor Lillenas

Chapter 7

Exposing the Critics

The reader may rest assured that this polemic will be challenged. Arguments will be presented such as Dr. Scrivener's who wrote that the Comma "is not found in any of the uncials (Scriptures written in Capitols), or any of the cursives, (Scriptures written in small letter) but a few ... not in the Peshitto, nor the best additions of the Harkleian, Sahidic, Bohairic, Ethiopic, Arabic...and scarcely any of the Armenian Codex...few recent Slavic copies and in the margin of the Moscow edition...."[61]

However, Dr. Scrivener, in his earlier writings in 1884, acknowledged that the Comma was found in the Peshitto. He, at that time, wrote that "it was unhappily thrust by the editors into the Peshito."[62] Without question, Dr. Scrivener, at times, is not consistent. Nevertheless, those who argue against the Comma say that it is found in only a few manuscripts and in a few ancient translations of the

---

61 (Scrivener, A Plain introduction to the New Testament Textual Criticism 402-403)
62 (Scrivener, Six Lectures on the Text of the New Testament 205)

In Defense of the Authenticity of 1 John 5:7

Scripture, with the exception of the Latin, where the witness is very strong. But he never had taken into consideration the historical struggle of the Greek Church with the Arians.

Therefore, in order to silence the testimony of the Latin manuscripts, Dr. Scrivener wrote, "It is only found in one fruitful branch of the church."[63] He was referring to the African church. The African church is but one branch of the church, and therefore, it is implied that there is no universal witness testifying to the disputed passage. Critics still use this argument to justify removal of the Comma. However, the Comma was, we have thus far established, found in the church universally.

At this time, the reader should observe several things that are revealing. The first observation is that the School of Higher Textual Criticism places far too much weight upon the older manuscripts. This has been addressed earlier, and now again it is repeated, even at the expense of being redundant. Yet once more we will touch upon this matter because many popular preachers and Bible teachers have been mesmerized by these early manuscripts, and especially so with the Sinaiticus and Vaticanus. But the truth remains, these older manuscripts are among the most corrupt.

At one time, Bible preachers and teachers were not even familiar with the above–named manuscripts since the textual critics of the past rejected these older manuscripts. This only shows how little these manuscripts were esteemed. Men like Desiderius Erasmus, Theodore Beza, Robert Stephens and others never considered those manuscripts that men presently esteem; they found them utterly worthless. But all this changed when unscrupulous men took it upon themselves to create a Bible of their own making. The only way they could achieve their end was to revive those

---

63 (Scrivener, Six Lectures on the Text of the New Testament 206)

manuscripts that were rejected by the church. Hence today, after so long a time, men have come to idolize these corrupt, heretical manuscripts our fathers earlier despised!

What, then, was the reasoning for this drastic change? How was it that this generation was led to accept the earlier dated manuscripts over the later–dated manuscripts? How were men ever able to convince the saints and even the world at large to accept corrupt manuscripts over those that were not corrupt? It is without question that the later—dated manuscripts are far, far superior to the earlier–dated manuscripts. Furthermore, the later–dated manuscripts were the ones the church universally used. That was why textual criticism for centuries ignored the earlier–dated manuscripts. But the question before us is how did this drastic change come about? How is it that the church has taken leave of its senses?

What has taken place is so astonishing that we are compelled to ask how these unscrupulous men were able to persuade the saints to accept absurdities. First, these men claim that the later–dated manuscripts were far more subject to error because of being transmitted from one generation to another. The more the Scriptures were copied, they reasoned, the more they were subject to error. In turn, the less they were copied, the less they were subject to error. This, of course, sounds reasonable; however, these critics ignore the providential hand of God preserving the truth. Our Lord said that He would preserve His Word to all generations (Ps. 12:6–7). The doctrine of the preservation of the Scriptures was ignored. Thus from the onset, it is apparent that the contemporary critics deny the supernatural.

Second, as previously stated, these unscrupulous men imply that the copyists would have a tendency to embellish the Scriptures. Thus, in compiling their Greek text, they set up laws to guide their judgments. As we have seen, these

In Defense of the Authenticity of 1 John 5:7

canons were no more than sophisticated emendations.[64] The two principles or laws set up to guide them were transcriptional probabilities and intrinsic probabilities. These are but absurdities at best. Take, for example, "transcriptional probabilities." These are speculative assumptions whereby the critic determines what the *author* would most likely have written! The second application of this principle is what the *copyist* would most likely have made the author seem to write! What the Scriptures actually say is ignored. Is this science or nonsense?

"Intrinsic probabilities" is another "principle" they have concocted. This canon is applied in deciding between two different readings. The decision is based upon the intuitive knowledge of the critic! Can anything be more subjective than this? These principles are stated in Westcott and Hort's *Introduction to the New Testament in the Original Greek,* on page 20 and following.[65] What a drastic change this is from copying the Greek manuscripts to that of composing an entirely new Bible! So now these modern-day critics have given us a Bible based upon the assumptions of men rather than "Thus saith the Lord"!

Furthermore, it had been kept back from the people, as well as most of the revisers on the committee, that these earlier manuscripts from which readings were taken were very corrupt manuscripts. In fact, those on the Revision Committee were not equipped to meet these challenges. They were not textual critics. They were to revise the Authorized Version, not create a new Bible. Later many, upon discovering the corruption of the two oldest manuscripts from which many of the changes were based, were outraged. Dr. Newth, a member on the committee, later wrote how many were duped and sat silent as Dr. Scrivener cast one

---

64 (Brooke F. Westcott and Fenton J. A. Hort 3)
65 (Brooke F. Westcott and Fenton J. A. Hort 20ff)

vote against changing a text, only to be outvoted by two. As for the other members on the committee, they were silent, as they were not qualified to meet the task that was suddenly thrust upon them.[66]

It may also interest the reader to learn that the Scriptures were more subject to corruption in the second and third century than at any other time in history. The Gnostics plagued the early church, so much so that the church in Rome was infected with more than a hundred heretical sects. The church in Rome was in such a deplorable state that Polycarp had to recall Irenaeus from the work in Gaul and send him to Rome. That was how deplorable the Church of Rome was. She was overwhelmed by Gnostic heretics.

Marcion of Sinopec, AD 140, was the most Christian of these Gnostics. He was also the most destructive of all the Gnostics, mutilating the Scriptures to the extreme. Philip Schaff gives one such example, arguing that "Marcion rejected all the books of the Old Testament, and wrested Christ's words in Matt. 5:17 into the very opposite declaration: I am come not to fulfill the Law and the prophets but to destroy them."[67] Being a man of great means, Marcion, through his school, inflicted enormous damage on the church in producing many corrupt copies of the Scriptures. He was not alone in violating the Sacred Text. There were many other Gnostics engaged in this same practice. But Marcion was the greatest menace in mutilating the Sacred Writ.

As strange as it may sound, the corrupting of the Scriptures also came from within the church. Men in the church, in seeking to correct the Scriptures, corrupted them. Dr. Edward F. Hills cites many examples of such corruptions that the Alexandrian School made. Origen, the founder of the school and one of the early church fathers, was notorious

---
66 (Fuller, True or False 90ff)
67 (Schaff, History of the Christian Church, Vol. 2 485)

In Defense of the Authenticity of 1 John 5:7

in corrupting the Holy Oracles. In seeking to correct the Scriptures, he actually did more damage. Dr. Hills gives us an example that will suffice in proving the point.

Dr. Hills wrote, "A specimen of the New Testament textual criticism which was carried on at Alexandria about AD 225. Origen reasoned that Jesus could not have concluded His list of God's commandments with the comprehensive requirement, *'Thou shalt love thy neighbor as thyself.'* For the reply of the young man was, *'all of these things I have kept from my youth up,'* and Jesus evidently accepted the statement as true. But if the young man had loved his neighbor as himself, he would have been perfect, for Paul says that the whole law is summed up in this saying, *'Thou shalt love thy neighbor as thyself.'* But Jesus answered, *'If thou wilt be perfect, etc.,* implying that the young man was not as yet perfect. Therefore Origen argued, that the commandment, *'Thou shalt love thy neighbor as thyself',* could not have been spoken by Jesus on this occasion and was not part of the original text of Matthew. This clause, he believed, was added by some tasteless scribe."[68] Therefore Origen omitted that portion of the Sacred Scriptures.

Thus we have a clear example where the Alexandrian School of Textual Criticism, in seeking to correct the Scriptures, corrupted them. Keep in mind that Eusebius, Origen's disciple, looked to Origen's works when he produced the fifty manuscripts of the New Testament ordered by Constantine. So much then for the acceptance of manuscripts merely upon their antiquity! The reader must never be carried away with these wiles. The oldest manuscripts are not the best. The very opposite is true; they are the worst! Thus, the Comma must not be omitted

---

68 Dr. Edward F. Hills, *The King James Defended* (Junction City, OR: Eye Opener Publishers, 1973), 144.

because of the testimony of the two oldest manuscripts. They are so corrupt that they should have never been considered!

As mentioned earlier, the dating of manuscripts is utterly foolish. A copy is a copy regardless of when it was copied. If a copy of the Original Autograph is of as late a date as 2010, it is just as valid as a copy dated AD 150. That is why we, who hold a copy of the Original Autograph in our own tongue, confess it is the Word of God and not that it contains the Word of God. The reader must never get carried away with the foolishness of dating manuscripts. Those who are caught up in such nonsense are those who deny the preservation of the Scriptures.

Another fact that should not be ignored is that the contemporary textual critics fail to separate the heretical manuscripts from the authentic. As mentioned earlier, they lump them all together! They are not concerned with so–called corrupt manuscripts. All the manuscripts are to be taken into consideration, catalogued, and divided into separate families or branches. Thus the corrupt copies of the Scriptures that were universally rejected by the saints are now used in producing their New Greek Text. This is alarming!

What makes this practice so appalling is that these few corrupt manuscripts that are compiled are given an equal witness to the 5,500 authentic Byzantine manuscripts. It is worth noting that the Byzantine manuscripts are the manuscripts that the church always used. A reader can readily discern the seriousness of the problem that has now been created. To simplify matters, let's pose a hypothetical situation. The Byzantine manuscripts bear witness to a particular reading. They serve as one witness. Now there is a second reading of the same passage from the corrupt Vaticanus and a few similar heretical manuscripts. These also are given an equal weight, as it is an opposing witness. Now we have a problem; which reading is to be accepted?

Thus a third reading is taken from another corrupt manuscript, such as the Sinaiticus and other like heretical manuscripts, on the same passage. These manuscripts represent another branch of the church. As it just so happens, this reading of the later two branches composed of heretical manuscripts are in agreement. Now what? The heretical manuscripts rule. Those heretical manuscripts that were formerly rejected by the church are presently incorporated into the Sacred Text. On the other hand, if the heretical manuscripts of these so-called two branches of the church omit a passage, then they rule, expunging a legitimate reading from the Byzantine text. Heresy now triumphs!

It is apparent that either the critics of the School of Higher Textual Criticism have taken leave of their senses or they have maliciously plotted to undermine the faith. The writer believes the latter is true. As for the Majority Text critics, they have gone to the absurd in seeking to collate ever extant manuscripts in order to produce what they call the Majority Greek Text. Presently we have two Majority Texts! Interesting! This will continue to be in flux as men discover and collate more manuscripts. Their final verdict is that we do not have an infallible Bible. If their position is to be accepted, then from the second century, we never had an infallible Bible. My how men still "strain at gnats and swallow camels"!

When our Lord spoke of preserving the Scriptures, He did not mean that He would preserve them in some clay earthen jars hidden in some desert caves. When our Lord spoke of preserving the Scriptures, it is to be understood that they would be preserved for men to read and know them. After all, did He not say, "Man shall not live by bread alone, *but by every word* that proceedeth out of the mouth of God"

(Matt. 4:4)? And again in John 12:48, He said, "He that rejecteth me, and receiveth not my words, hath one that judgeth him: the word that I have spoken, the same shall judge him in the last day." If the only manuscripts that are assumed to be credible are tenth century or older, as the contemporary critics claim, then what shall we say of the Scriptures the saints embraced for the past one thousand years! Enough of the so–called early manuscripts! They survived only because they were not used. They were not used because they were heretical.

Also, the reader should perceive how the School of Higher Textual Critics refers to different branches or families of the church. This is apparent in Dr. Scrivener's writings. This principle was set before the Revision Committee by Westcott and Hort. However, Dr. Scrivener is mentioned because he unequivocally refers to the different branches of the church. For example, he wrote of the Comma as "belonging *to one fruitful branch of the church and no other.*"[69] It is important that the reader take note of what was said. The reader should consider these words in particular, *"One fruitful branch of the church."* This thought was punctuated with the words, *"And no other."* No other what? No other branches of the church!

Notice how these textual critics, through their craftiness, divide the church and the Scriptures into families or into different branches. Each branch of the church had its own particular version of what is called Scripture. The critics' task, as they saw it, was to compile readings from these different sources and produce a Bible. Thus the number of witnesses to a particular passage is not important. That which is essential is the agreement of these different sources (branches) on a given passage, as earlier mentioned.

---

69 (Scrivener, Six Lectures on the Text of the New Testament 205)

For example, Westcott and Hort wrote that if nine manuscripts agree with each other, they must be reduced to one single witness. The reasoning is that they all came from one common source. If one manuscript disagrees with the nine, then both have equal weight. This is because the nine represent one source and the one in disagreement represents another source. Numbers are meaningless. The only importance is that different sources agree with each other *(Introduction to the New Testament Greek,* pp. 20 ff).

What is alarming is the foundation upon which the School of Higher Textual Criticism rests. It rests upon *Source or Form Criticism.* These are two different terms describing the same school of thought. This school denies divine revelation and preservation of the Scriptures. They treat the Holy Bible as nothing more than ancient literature. By the nineteenth century, those men of this school had set aside all efforts to fill ancient religion with direct meaning and relevance and devoted themselves instead to the critical collection and chronological ordering of the source materials. The Liberal German School was the first to apply this method of criticism to the Bible.

For example, they affirm that the Pentateuch, as it stands today, was derived from supposedly four different sources over a period of about 550 years. The letters J, E, D, and P are letters used to designate each of these sources from which the Pentateuch was compiled. The "J" source is supposedly the oldest source. The supposed scholars date it about 950 BC. At this time, the kingdom of Israel was established, and the nation began to worship God as Jehovah.

Then there is the "E" or the Elohim source. This source these supposed scholars associated with establishment of the Northern Kingdom. The Northern Kingdom broke with the religion of the Southern Kingdom, and they began to refer to God as Elohim. So now we have a second source from which the Pentateuch was compiled. This source is said to have come into existence about 750 BC.

Then there is the supposed "D" or Deuteronomy source, which they arbitrarily dated around 650 BC. This is the time of King Josiah's reign. When King Josiah came into power, he ushered in a great reformation in Judah, the Southern Kingdom. It is supposed that at this time there was the second giving of the Law. Therefore, they refer to this period as the Deuteronomy Reform. It was at this time, they assumed, the book of Deuteronomy was written.

As for the "P" or Priest source, it did not come into existence until sometime after the fall of the Southern Kingdom, which they date 587 BC. It was another 187 years later, around 400 BC, that all these sources were finally compiled and edited by the priests. It was at that time the Pentateuch as we know it was completed.[70] (Source critics vary on the date by one or two centuries.)

It is apparent that the school of Source or Form Criticism denies divine revelation. They deny that the source of all Scriptures is God Himself. They deny divine revelation and inspiration of the Scriptures. They actually mock the plain declaration, "God, who at sundry times and in divers manners spake in time past unto the fathers by the prophets, Hath in these last days spoken unto us by his Son, whom he hath appointed heir of all things, by whom also he made the worlds" (Heb. 1:1–2). They say that God did not speak to men but rather men at different times had a different concept of God and these sources of ancient literature over 550 years were finally put together by the priests in 400 or 500 BC to give us the Pentateuch.

When Bible believers challenged these men to explain the prophecies and their fulfillment, they came up with

---

70 Bernard W. Anderson, *Understanding the Old Testament* (London: Prentice-Hall International Inc, 1966), 16-17.

concocted answers. For example, G. Earnest Wright and Regina H. Fuller, in their work, *The Book of the Acts of God*, address this very question. The Prophets, they said, "expounded the relevant word of God for their particular times and any visions of the future to which they gave utterance were projections from the known past and present situations."[71] Thus God did not speak to the fathers by the prophets. The prophets, by their own evaluation of situations based upon past experiences and present situations, made their so–called prophetic utterances that were no more than mere predictions. There is nothing supernatural in that. But then, they deny the supernatural.

"Source" or "Form Criticism" laid the foundation for the School of Higher Textual Criticism. It is upon this foundation that the School of Higher Textual Criticism actually rests. This foundation explains why the critics of this School of Higher Textual Criticism speak of different branches of the church. These different branches are said to be different sources from which materials were gathered and assimilated in making up the Critical Greek New Testament. What these form critics did with the Old Testament, the School of Higher Textual Criticism did to the New Testament. The Greek Bible of the New Critical Text rests upon this pseudo–scholarship.

For example, source critics suppose that the gospel of Mark is the earliest of the gospels. Upon the death of Peter, Mark is said to have taken upon himself to write the stories of Jesus as he heard them from Peter. These stories of miracles were embellishments on the writer's part, "As for raising Jarius' daughter from the dead, she was in a coma and later awakened."[72] As for, "Matthew and Luke, they

---

71 G Ernest Wright and Reginald h. Fuller, *The Acts of God* (Garden City, NY: Double Day & Co., 1957), 144-145.

72 (Wainwright 31)

edited Mark's material and combined it with narratives and sayings from other sources."[73] According to these critics, the Scriptures are not divine revelation but rather the fruitful invention of men. No Christian would ever accept such nonsense.

The reader should observe how that word "source" or "sources" frequently comes up in the speech of these writers. It is a term used to describe from whence the Scriptures were acquired. According to them, the Scriptures were acquired and not revealed. These men of the School of Higher Textual Criticism "acquired" materials to invent the Critical Greek Text. This is not an assumption but an inescapable fact. Regardless of how much one likes one's New American Standard Bible or the New International Version or any of these new translations, whatever they might be, they are all the product of these source critics who deny divine revelation, inspiration, and the preservation of Scripture.

This is a serious charge. Can it be substantiated? Indeed it can. Consider Dr. Bruce M. Metzger, one of the leading textual critics of the twenty–first century and one of the most esteemed editors of the Critical Greek New Testament published by the United Bible Society. He wrote:

> At times reverence for the Bible has been carried to such a point that any critical study of its books was frowned upon. But when it is found that some traditional views of the authorship and dates of certain books have been ill–grounded, it is not irreverent to seek for another interpretation that will do full justice to the facts of the Scripture. By such methods several traditional opinions have been virtually overthrown; for example, the Pentateuch is no

---

[73] (Wainwright 29)

longer attributed to the personal authorship of Moses but ascribed to a much later period in the history of Israel (probably the ninth through the 5th century BC). In the New Testament the differences in the historical value between the Gospels According to John and the other three synoptic gospels are generally acknowledged. It is now recognized that reverent and critical study of the language of the Bible, its thought, and its background can only lead to a fuller understanding of its essential message.[74]

But Dr. Metzger is not alone on this matter. This was the mindset of the revisionists who revised the Authorized Version. Dr. Stanly, one of the many liberals on the Revision committee, openly said: "I might mention on who … has ventured to say that the Pentateuch is not the work of Moses … who has ventured to say that the narratives of those historical incidents are colored not unfrequently by the necessary infirmities which belong to the human instruments by which they convey—and that individual is the one who now addresses you."[75]

The writer at this time would like to pose a question. If Moses did not write the Pentateuch, as Dr. Metzger, Dr. Stanly, Dr. Colenso, and others affirm so emphatically, what then are we to make of the words of our Lord Jesus, who said, "For had ye believed Moses, ye would have believed me: for he wrote of me" (John 5:46)? Was our Lord mistaken? Was He carried away with the whims of the times? Or was He merely accommodating the superstition of the Jews of those days? To suggest anything of this nature is to deny

---

[74] Reader's Digest Association, *The Bible Through the Ages* (Pleasantville, NY: Reader's Digest Inc., 1996), 13.
[75] (Fuller, Which Bible 296)

the deity of our Lord. This was the reason some of the revisionists challenged the Comma; they just openly denied the deity of Christ Jesus.

The issue before us is obvious: it is *not* a matter of a preference of a translation. The issue is a battle for the Bible! If one text can be removed from the Scriptures, who is to say that another shall not be removed? What shall restrain these men from removing all the passages that are presently in brackets? If our Lord Jesus tarries, no doubt in time all of those passages will be removed. It is just a matter of time. Of the Comma, Dr. Scrivener writes, "The authenticity of the words within the brackets will, perhaps no longer be maintained ...."[76] He was right. The Comma was first placed in brackets. Now it has been altogether removed from the Critical Editions of the New Testament. In time, the others will follow. Is there any reason to think otherwise?

No longer are the Scriptures revered as the "Voice from Beyond." They are no longer regarded as the very Word of God. Professors in our schools and universities present the Bible to young scholars as fables of ancient literature. The source critics have accomplished their end. They are rightly defined as *"Unholy Hands on the Holy Bible."*[77] Presently, pastors in many churches are correcting the Scriptures rather than correcting the people by the Scriptures.

As an example of irreverence, as recently as 2009, the Gideons were passing out Bibles to the students just outside a local high school. The students would take them and walk away, laughing and throwing them on the ground. The police were later called, and the Gideons were forced to leave.

---

[76] (Scrivener, A Plain introduction to the New Testament Textual Criticism 401)

[77] John W. Burgan-Green, *An Introduction to Textual Criticism* (Lafayette, IN: Sovereign Grace Trust Fund, 1990) 1.

In Defense of the Authenticity of 1 John 5:7

By God's grace, there is a faithful remnant who fears the Lord and follows the Lamb. Those of the true faith treasure the Scriptures, hiding His Word in their hearts that they might not sin against God (Ps. 119:11). However, deceitful men, through their wiles, are seeking to wrest the Word of God from the hearts of saints, and it is for these saints that this work is set forth. It is with the purpose to strengthen them to continue in the truth, looking patiently for the return of our Lord Jesus Christ. Together we must strive in our Christian walk, seeking to please our Heavenly Father and lead men to a saving knowledge of Him, which is through faith in our Lord Jesus Christ. And when life's journey ends, we may be received with joy into the Celestial City.

Nevertheless, there is a second reason for this work; it is to expose the lie. The so–called scholars are no scholars but rather deceivers. They need to be exposed. Yes, the emperor is indeed naked! He has no clothes!

> Break Thou the bread of life, Dear Lord, to me,
> As Thou didst break the loaves Beside the sea;
> Beyond the Sacred Page I seek Thee, Lord;
> My Spirit pants for Thee, O Living Word.
>
> Bless Thou the truth dear Lord To me, to me
> As Thou didst bless the bread By Galilee;
> Then shall all bondage cease, All fetters fall;
> And I shall find my peace, My All in All.
>
> Thou art the Bread of Life, O Lord to me,
> Thy holy Word the truth That saveth me;
> Give me to eat and live With Thee above; Teach me to love Thy Truth, For Thou art love.

O send Thy Spirit, Lord, Now unto me,
That He may touch mine eyes, And make me see: Show me the truth concealed With–in Thy Word, And in Thy Book revealed I see the Lord.

–Mary Ann Lathbury

CHAPTER 8

THE REVISION COMMITTEES

I have often wondered why those who supposedly revised the Holy Scriptures are referred to as "Committees." A committee consists of those who are appointed. May I ask who appointed these men? As for those who worked upon the Revised Version, some may argue that the Anglican Church appointed them.[78] But is this true? Dr. Scrivener writes that the project was under the Auspices of the Convocation of the province of Canterbury. This was true in the inception but they cast off the rules by which they were to carry out the work thus divorcing themselves from the auspices of the church.

Also, those who were to revise the Scriptures in Britain were only to be Churchmen, but this was not the case as earlier pointed out. Furthermore, this group appealed to the Americans to work with them in revising the Sacred Scriptures. Thus, an additional thirty men from various denominations worked together on this project, and the

---

78 Frederick H. A. Scrivener, *The Authorized Version of the English Bible* (Edinburgh, England: Cambridge University Press, 2010), 1.

revision of the Scriptures became a joint project of the British and the Americans. They had finished the work at the same time. However, for profit motives, the Revised Version was published first, and then the American Standard Bible followed ten years later.

It is, therefore, obvious that these men who revised the Sacred Scriptures were men working outside the church. Is it any wonder that these revisions of the Bible were not accepted by the church? Of the Revised Version, Dr. Scrivener said it would take at least one if not two generations before it would be accepted.[79]

In regard to the American Standard Version, it was also rejected by the Church. Dr. Schaff was delighted when the American Council of Churches accepted the work, but who are they? The American Council of Churches is not the church of God which is "the pillar and ground of the truth" (1 Timothy 3:15).

As for Dr. Philip Schaff, he unequivocally denied the inspiration of the Scripture, even in the Original Autograph. He wrote *The History of the Christian Church* and headed up the so–called Committee of The American Standard Version of the Bible. Some have said this was his greatest work, although he claimed he had put far more labor into the former. What the reader must not fail to grasp is that this man, who was tried twice for heresy, is attributed to producing the American Standard Version. It is said to be chiefly the work of a heretic!

Dr. Schaff not only headed The Committee of The American Standard Version of the Bible, but he also selected the men who were to revise the Scriptures. He carefully chose them from several different denominations. All of these men whom he had chosen were of the same persuasion;

---

[79] (Scrivener, The Authorized Version of the English Bible 1)

they too did not hold to the inspiration of the Original Autograph. If they did, Dr. Schaff undoubtedly would never have selected them.

One of the men on the Committee whom he highly praised was Joseph Henry Thayer, D. D. Of him, Dr. Schaff said that he had labored more fervently on the revision than any other. Joseph Henry Thayer was a devout Unitarian who denied the deity of our Lord Jesus Christ. Thus, we have men outside the church meddling with the Bible. Is it any wonder that the Church never accepted these translations!

What is of further interest is that the Jehovah's Witnesses embraced the American Standard Bible until the 1960's. It was at that time the Jehovah's Witnesses (Watch Tower) started publishing their own Bible. Today, supposed conservatives embrace this same Bible. Although it is presently referred to as the New American Standard Version, there is nothing new about it, as it has become more abominable. It is amazing how the unacceptable became acceptable!

Christians that like to think of themselves as defenders of the truth, confess that the Original Autograph was inspired. This is most certainly true but that does not go far enough. What does such a confession have to say of the Bible that we have in our hands? Nothing! This is because we do not have the Original Autograph. From this empty confession, deceived men have come to embrace the new corrupt translations of the Bible. They have failed to acknowledge the divine preservation of the Scriptures.

For centuries, preachers of the gospel unequivocally held to the Authorized Version affirming that it is the inspired, infallible Word of God. This is the position taken by true Christians to this day. How else can they preach, "Thus saith the Lord"? Alas, although contemporary Christians have surrendered the authority of the Scriptures to the authority of pseudo–scholars, true believers are people of the Book. They stand upon, "Thus saith the LORD." May our Lord bring us to our senses!

> Supposed Scholars–nonsense babel!
> Denying God's Word–the Holy Bible.
> They choke on the word Infallible.
> To them the thought is intolerable!
>
> Yet throughout the rages of time,
> The Word of God still stands sublime.
> Foes have come–and fallen away
> But God's Word, is here to stay!

Appeal to the Reader

Our Lord warned, when good men sleep, wicked men sow their tares (Matt. 13:25). In one sense, good men have fallen asleep and are now with the Lord. These were godly men who held without compromise to the Authorized Version of the Scriptures. They faithfully warned their congregations to resist all the new translations of Scripture that were flooding the market. They fought the good fight of faith, resisting and exposing those corrupt versions of the Bible. However, these men are no longer with us. They have been called home. They have laid down their armor and entered into their rest.

The responsibility of carrying on the good fight of faith presently rests upon our shoulders. All who have come to know our Lord Jesus Christ are to put on the whole armor of God and after doing all, to stand (Eph. 6:13). It is we who are exhorted to "earnestly contend for the faith which was once delivered unto the saints" (Jude 3). This exhortation was not given to a select few but to each and every person who is a member of the household of God. We, collectively as one man with Christ as our Head, are to earnestly contend for the faith. The warfare has not passed. It still rages. And it shall rage until our great God and Savior shall appear. Until then, we are to be faithfully engaged in the struggle against the darkness that strives to extinguish the light.

The contending for the preservation of the Scriptures is no small matter. Consider if those early saints did not contend for the Scriptures as they did, where would we be today? It is true that our Lord Jesus preserves the Scriptures, but He does so through faithful men. And those men and women of the third century as we have gathered, as well as those down through the centuries, laid down their lives rather than surrender the Holy Oracles into wicked hands. And yes, there were traitors who handed the Scriptures over to be destroyed, but we do not wish to be numbered with that infamous crowd. Shall we rest on beds of ease when others so valiantly fought the fight to hand down to us the pure Word of God?

One then might inquire, "How am I to contend for the faith? What can I do about the proliferation of these heretical versions of Scriptures that flood the market? I am not a scholar, pastor, or Bible teacher! I am just an average person sitting in the pew supporting my church and seeking the salvation of my acquaintances. How am I to actively contend for the faith other than doing what I am presently doing?"

The first thing we all can do is not to purchase any of these heretical versions of the Scriptures. The writer is aware that there are Christians who purchase them in order to compare readings. Many are engaged in this practice in hope of gaining more light on a given passage. We must not do that but rather give ourselves to prayer. After all, did not our Lord promise to send the Comforter to teach us all things (John 14:26)? Therefore, we must depend upon our Lord and not lean upon these bruised reeds of Egypt that will pierce us through (2 Kings 18:21). Just the thought of looking to heretical writings for light is quite troublesome!

In Defense of the Authenticity of 1 John 5:7

Second, we must inform those we know about the seriousness of this matter so they will not purchase any of these new translations of the Scriptures. They need someone to show them the truth. Who can better do that than you, their friend? Unless men come to know the truth, they cannot resist the evils that confront them. Remember, ye are the light of the world and the salt of the earth (Matt. 5:13–14). A light is not lit to be placed under a basket, but rather it is lit to be placed upon a stand to lighten the entire house (Matt. 5:15). In other words, "Let your light so shine before men, that they may see your good works, and glorify your Father which is in heaven" (Matt. 5:16).

One may ask the question, "What should I do if my pastor is using one of these new translations of the Bible?" It is our duty to pray for our pastors. A pastor is a man just as we. It is our duty not only to pray for him, but it is also our duty to inform him of the truth. Remember, he most likely had been subjected to heretical teachers. As a young man in seminary, he may have had a professor who took advantage of his youth and led him astray. It is with meekness he is to be approached, and perhaps God will grant him repentance (2 Tim. 2:25).

Neither should we be hesitant in approaching our pastor if he is using a heretical translation of the Scriptures. Love demands us to go to him. As yet we do not have popes, priests, and bishops ruling over us. May our Lord deliver us from such tyrants! Our authority is the Word of God. It is upon the Scriptures we take our stand. All authorities must bow before the Sacred Oracles, for we shall all be judged by them (John 12:48). With confidence, approach your pastor in meekness, and if his eyes are opened, he will be forever indebted to you.

But one might ask, "What should I do if my pastor does not change? What if he adamantly cleaves to the New

Critical Greek Text and those new translations of the Bible?" Well, what does our Lord say? Did He not say, "Know ye not that a little leaven leaveneth the whole lump?" (1 Cor. 5:6). This is an admonition few have taken seriously. Falling away is not necessarily something that comes about suddenly but, in most cases, is gradual.

The writer knows of saints who were members of a particular church for over fifty years. When their new pastor came into the pulpit, he preached from a modern version of the Scriptures. They were stunned at first and later made an appointment to see him. They faithfully informed him of his error, but he would not hear. Hence, as they saw it, there was only one thing for them to do; find another church. It was with broken hearts that they left the church in which they served for more than fifty years. They also left many of their friends behind. But in time, many of them also came out seeking another church.

Others remained in the church faithfully praying for their pastor to have his eyes opened. Are they compromising? We are not to judge. The writer recalls in years past conversing with Sister Bertha Smith. For those who may not be acquainted with her, she served as a missionary from her youth in China. At the age of seventy–five, the mission board called her home. She did not want to come home, but she did. However, she did not cease laboring for the Lord. In our conversation, she said that she sat on the third row from the front in her church. She went on to say that she kept her eyes upon her pastor praying in earnest for his conversion! Was she wrong? No, she knew something of the power of prayer. After all, she discovered in China many of the missionaries with which she labored were later saved in those wonderful visitations of our Lord. However, there are ever so few who know anything of fasting and prayer.

In Defense of the Authenticity of 1 John 5:7

An argument that is often presented is that the Authorized Version is very difficult to understand. Upon this premise, men have dumbed down the Bible. In some cases, it is even produced in a comic book form. However, we do not find men coming to know the Lord or understanding the Scriptures any better through these dumbed–down versions of the Scriptures. This is because the problem is not with the Scriptures. The problem is with the individual. Men must be born again before they can come to understand the Word of God. Have we not read, "But the natural man receiveth not the things of the Spirit of God: for they are foolishness unto him: neither can he know them, because they are spiritually discerned" (1 Cor. 2:14)?

Last, in contending for the faith, we must not resort, as some have, to burning these new translations of the Scriptures. This is utterly foolish. This is not the way we are to address the problem. Our prayer and aim should be to inform the populace so they will destroy their own heretical Bibles, and also by informing them, they will cease to purchase these heretical versions of the Bible. If we succeed, then by the grace of God, these corrupt versions of the Scriptures will cease to be published. It is sad but the truth is, if it does not sell, then it will not be printed. The publishers publish for profit. It would be wonderful if men with convictions would cease to publish these heretical versions of the Bible. But this will never happen unless we earnestly contend for the faith. May there be again a cry of outrage not only because of the removal of the Trinitarian passage but also because of the mutilation of the entire Bible.

Brethren, these are troubling times. A new generation has come on the scene that has removed the old landmarks (Job 24:2). The older generation knows better, but some are making compromise, to their hurt. With age there is often a tendency to relax. We must remember we are running a race and we are not to relax until we cross the finish line (1 Cor. 9:24). May we say, as the apostle Paul, when our journey is through, "I have fought a good fight, I have finished my course, I have kept the faith: Henceforth there is laid up for me a crown of righteousness, which the Lord, the righteous judge, shall give me at that day: and not to me only, but unto all them also that love his appearing" (2 Tim. 4:7–8).

In contending for the faith, we must never grow cold in our love for our Lord Jesus Christ. Our desire is to magnify Him before all men, that they too might be drawn unto Him. Thus, Jude closes his exhortation with these words, which is a proper closing to this exhortation as well: "Keep yourselves in the love of God, looking for the mercy of our Lord Jesus Christ unto eternal life. And of some have compassion, making a difference: And others save with fear, pulling them out of the fire; hating even the garment spotted by the flesh. Now unto him that is able to keep you from falling, and to present you faultless before the presence of his glory with exceeding joy, To the only wise God our Saviour, be glory and majesty, dominion and power, both now and ever. Amen" Jude 21–25).

May our Lord Jesus Christ be ever glorified, Amen.

Appendix

The witness of the Church Fathers

At this time some of the church fathers are summoned that testify in behalf of the Comma. There is **Athenagorus of Athens, (AD 177)**. He referred to the Trinitarian passage when he wrote in his, *Plea for the Christians:* "Who, then, would not speak of God the Father, and of God the Son, and of the Holy Spirit, and who declare both their power in union and in their distinction in order…" Ante Nicene Fathers, Vol. II New York NY, 1913, Charles Scribner's Sons. P. 133

Tertullian, AD 215–in his apologetic work *Against Praxeas* wrote, *"Thus the connection of the Father in the Son, and of the Son in the Paraclete, produces three coherent Persons, who are yet distinct One from Another. These Three are one essence, not one Person, as it is said, 'I and my Father are One,' in respect of unity of substance not singularity of number."* Tertullian, *Against Praxeas*, Ch. 25 Ante Nicene Fathers Vol. III p. 621

Cyprian AD 250 *'I and the Father are one' and likewise it is written of the Father and the Son and the Holy Spirit, 'And these three are one'.* Ante Nicene Fathers, Vol. V, p.423

Athanasius AD 350 also attests to the Comma. He wrote, *"Fulgentius, in the beginning of the "sixth" century, against the Arians, without any scruple or hesitation; and Jerom, as before observed, has it (the Comma) in his translation made in the latter end of the "fourth" century; and it (the Comma) is cited by Athanasius about the year 350; and before him by Cyprian in the middle of the "third" century, about 250; and is referred to by Tertullian about the year 200; and which was within a "hundred" years, or little more, of the writing of the epistle; which may be enough to satisfy anyone of the genuineness of this passage;"*. John Gill in his commentary on 1 John 5:7.

Gregory of Nazianzus AD 379 of the Greek Church testified to the Comma in his Oration 32, The Fifth Theological Oration, On the Holy Spirit, Para. 19. (Note also chapter 4, pp.48 ff)

Varimadum AD 380 wrote, "And there are three who give testimony in heaven, the Father, the Word, and the Spirit, and these three are one", Varimadum 90:20–21.

Priscillian of Spain in AD 385 wrote, *"and there are three which give testimony on earth, the water, the flesh, the blood, and these three are in one, and there are three which give testimony in heaven, the Father, the Word, and the Spirit, and these three are one in Christ Jesus"* Liber Apologeticus. (Note chapter 1 p.15)

Jerome, AD347 – 420, *In the prologue to the Canonical Epistles; from the prologue appended to Codex Fludensis we read, "Just as these are properly understood and so translated faithfully by interpreters into Latin without leaving ambiguity for the readers nor [allowing] the variety of genres to conflict, especially in that text where **we read the unity of the trinity***

is placed in the first letter of John, where much error has occurred at the hands of unfaithful translators contrary to the truth of faith, who have kept just the three words water, blood and spirit in this edition omitting mention of Father, Word and Spirit in which especially the catholic faith is strengthened and the unity of substance of Father, Son and Holy Spirit is attested."

Augustine, AD 354–430, concerning 1 John 5:8, leaned heavily upon the Comma. He wrote, *"I would not have thee mistake that place in the epistle of John the apostle where he saith, 'There are three witnesses: the spirit, and the water, and the blood: and the three are one.' Lest haply thou say that the Spirit and the water and the blood are diverse substances, and yet it is said, 'the three are one:' for this cause I have admonished thee, that thou mistake not the matter. For these are mystical expressions, in which the point always to be considered is, not what the actual things are, but what they denote as signs: since they are signs of things, and what they are in their essence is one thing, what they are in their signification another. If then we understand the things signified, we do find these things to be of one substance. Thus, if we should say, the rock and the water are one, meaning by the Rock, Christ; by the water, the Holy Ghost: who doubts that rock and water are two different substances? Yet because Christ and the Holy Spirit are of one and the same nature, therefore when one says, the rock and the water are one, this can be rightly taken in this behalf, that these two things of which the nature is diverse, are signs of other things of which the nature is one. Three things then we know to have issued from the Body of the Lord when He hung upon the tree: first, the Spirit: of which it is written, 'And He bowed the head and gave up the spirit:' then, as His side was pierced by the spear, 'blood and water.' Which three things if we look at as they are in themselves, they are in substance several and distinct, and therefore they are not one. But if we will inquire into the* *things signified I by these, there not unreasonably comes into our thought the Trinity itself, which is the One, Only, True, Supreme God, Father and Son and Holy Ghost, of whom it could most truly be said, 'There are Three Witnesses, and the Three are One:' so that by the term Spirit we should understand God the Father to be signified; as indeed it was concerning the worshipping of Him that the Lord was speaking, when He said, 'God is a Spirit:' by the term, blood, the Son; because 'the Word was made flesh:' and by the term water, the Holy Ghost; as, when Jesus spake of the water which He would give to them that thirst, the evangelist saith, 'But this said He of the Spirit which they that believed on Him were to receive.' Moreover, that the Father, Son, and Holy Ghost are 'Witnesses,' who that believes the Gospel can doubt, when the Son saith, 'I am one that bear witness of myself, and the Father that sent me, He beareth witness of me.' Where, though the Holy Ghost is not mentioned, yet He is not to be thought separated from them. Howbeit neither concerning the Spirit hath He kept silence elsewhere, and that He too is a witness hath been sufficiently and openly shown. For in promising Him He said, 'He shall bear witness of me.' These are the Three Witnesses, and the Three are One, because of one substance. But whereas, the signs by which they were signified came forth from the Body of the Lord, herein they figured the Church preaching the Trinity, that it hath one and the same nature: since these Three in threefold manner signified are One, and the Church that preacheth them is the Body of Christ. I this manner then the three things by which they are signified came out from the Body: of the Lord: like as from the Body of the Lord sounded forth the command to 'baptize the nations in the Name of the Father and of the Son and of the Holy Ghost.' 'In the name:' not, In the names: for 'these Three are One,' and One God is these Three. And if in any other way is depth of mystery which we read in John's epistle can be expounded and understood agreeably with the*

Catholic faith, which neither confounds nor divides the Trinity, neither believes the substances diverse nor denies that the persons are three, it is on no account to be rejected. For whenever in Holy Scriptures in order to exercise the minds of the faithful anything is put darkly, it is to be joyfully welcomed if it can be in many ways but not unwisely expounded," Augustine, *Against Maximinium*, Bk. 2, Ch. 22.3

Much length has been given to Augustine because it is said he knew nothing of the Comma. However it is apparent that Augustine interpreted 1 John 5:8 in context of 1 John 5:7. Although he was addressing verse eight at the time, he did so in the context of verse seven as indicated by the bold print in the quoted passages above. Augustine quotes the masculine participle in his argument μαρτυρυντες which refers to the witnesses of the Father, the Word and the Spirit of the seventh verse.

Then there are a host of other Church Fathers we shall mention quickly. There is Cassian (AD 435), Cassiodorus (AD 580), and a host of other African and Western bishops in subsequent centuries have cited the Comma. Speculum (or M of AD 450), Victor Vitensis (AD 485), Victor of Vita (AD 489), Codes Freisingensis (of AD 500), Fulgentius (AD 533), Isidore of Seville (AD 636), Codex Pal Legionensis (AD 650), and Jaqub of Edessa (AD 700). Interestingly, it is also found in the edition of the Apostle's Creed used by the Waldenses and Albigensians of the twelfth century. Some are of the opinion that St. Augustine was the author of the Speculum.

Thus the church fathers in Spain, Greece, Rome and Africa quoted the Trinitarian passage. As for the omission of the Comma in many Greek Manuscripts, and also not quoted by more Church Father, Dr John Gill in his commentary on 1 John 5:7 wrote: *"thought not in the copies used by them, through the carelessness or unfaithfulness of transcribers; or it might be in their copies, and yet not cited by them, they having Scriptures enough without it, to defend the doctrine of the Trinity, and the divinity of Christ: and yet, after all, certain it is, that it is cited by many of them;"* John Gill Commentary on 1 John 5:7. Then Dr. Gill proceeded to cite many fathers that testify to the Comma. Hence the historical witness of the church in regard to the Comma is universal.

The Arian Persecutions

History should not be divorced from the controversy surrounding the Comma. For example, one of the reasons for the Comma's absence in the early Germanic and Slavic translations of the Holy Scriptures was because these groups were evangelized by Arians. These Germanic tribes were called Vandals, from which we get our word vandalism. Remember, the Arian heretics controlled the Greek Church for a long time. While they were in power, they evangelized the Germanic nations that in turn became Arians. Even after Arians were no longer in power, they continued for centuries to do a great deal of harm.

Dr. Philip Schaff writes of the consequences that followed even after the Arians lost their hold on the Greek Church. He wrote, "From that time it lost its importance as a Politico–Theological power, but continued as an uncatholic sect more than 200 years among the Germanic nations which were converted under Arian domination."[80]

The reader should take note that for two hundred years, these Germanic tribes were converted under the Arian power. Is it any wonder that their early translations of the Sacred Scriptures had the omission of the Comma? What is also appalling is these ancient translations are brought forth

---

80 (Schaff, History of the Christian Church, Vol. 3 619)

as witnesses against the Comma. These men are not honest, as they hide the historical events from the people in order to sell their cheap merchandise!

The situation became even more acute when in AD456; Genseric the vandal conquered North Africa. He then proceeded to take Hippo, where Augustine had shortly been appointed bishop. It was in that thirteen–month siege of Hippo that Augustine, being eighty–five, died. Although they fought valiantly, they were finally overcome by famine and diseases. King Genseric, being an Arian, persecuted those who were orthodox in their theology. He expelled all the bishops from their churches who would not embrace the heretical teachings of Arianism.

In AD 476, Rome fell into his hands, and shortly thereafter, his son, Hunneric, became king. Hunneric's persecution of the saints was exceedingly cruel and much more so than that of his father. He persecuted all *Homoousians,* as they were called. Many historians refer to the *Homoousians* as Catholics. Actually, the meaning of the Greek word is that the Son is *the same* in substance and essence as that of the Father. Hence, the Son is very God as the Father is very God; they are equally God.

The Arians, on the other hand, were *Homoiousia's,* meaning the Son was of *like or of similar* to the Father. The Son was a second God but not equal to God the Father. The controversy centered around the terms the *"same"* and *"like."* Their concept of our Lord Jesus was the same as that of the Jehovah's Witnesses, Unitarians, and Mormons of our day. They taught and believed that God created or begat the Son by eternal generation and the Son in turn created all things. Therefore, the Son is not very God. He is like God, but He is not God. Is it any wonder that they rejected 1 John 5:7 that asserts that the Father, Word, and Spirit are one!

The Arians, who evangelized the Vandals, no doubt omitted the Comma in their translation of the Scriptures, even as the Jehovah's Witnesses and other Arians do to this day. Man has not changed; he is the same. We should not be surprised that the wicked continue to mutilate the Scriptures. Nor should we be startled to discover that the Arians of old also did the same as those men of the School of Higher Textual Criticism presently do.

That with which the reader should be acquainted is the Reign of King Hunneric. He unmercifully persecuted all Homoousians. He not only made the bishops give up their churches and turned them over to Arian bishops, but he also sent these bishops to beg in order to survive. If any were caught giving food or shelter to these *Homoousians* bishops, they would be burned with their entire families.

As for the people who would not come over to the Arian heresy, they were maimed of either hand or foot or nose or even worse, they were put to death. Some even had their eyes put out, left to wander in darkness. Neither was anyone allowed to give them food or shelter. If anyone was caught showing compassion to these suffering saints, their life and the lives of their families would be forfeited.

The Homoousians, the true saints, suffered immensely after the fall of the Roman Empire. No less than five thousand bishops, priests, and deacons perished. Also, many saints who were true to the faith were maimed and left to wander from place to place in search for food and shelter. Yet, there remained a faithful witness of Waldensians who dwelt in the rugged mountains of the Alps. They had the Scriptures and evangelized Europe.

It is important that the reader is enlightened to the historical crises in the church at that particular time. It will help him or her to understand why the Comma was omitted from some of the early translations of the Scriptures. History must not be divorced from the issue that is at hand, as nothing just happens. There are always causes and effects in every area of life.

Two Greek Texts

Often we hear pastors say, "In the Greek it reads thus and thus," and in most instances the readings are different than the reading in our Authorized Version. This leaves the saint in the pew confused. What the reader should be cognizant of is that there are two different Greek Texts. One is the "*Critical Greek Text*," and the other is the "*Received Greek Text*." It is from these two different Greek Texts all of our translations of the Scriptures are produced.

The Authorized Version was translated from the *Received Greek Text*. This is the Greek Text that was always used by the churches throughout the ages. The *Critical Greek Text* is a modern invention that came into existence of late. Thus all of these new translations of the Scriptures that are flooding the market are translated from the *Critical Greek Text*. This is with the exception of the New King James New Testament. But as to the Old Testament, the New Kings James is not to be received, as it is divorced from the Hebrew Mesoretic Text.

There are pastors who are seeking to lead their congregations to receive these new translations of the Scriptures. They are deceiving them saying that there is no difference between their new translations of the Scriptures and the Authorized Version. But nothing is further from the truth. As for these two different Greek New Testaments, the Critical Greek Text and the Received Greek Text, there is a drastic difference between them. Just in the New Testament alone there are almost six thousand differences and variations between the two. One example is the Received Text contains the Comma; the Critical Text omits it altogether.

When the writer studied Greek in seminary, he had to purchase the Greek New Testament produced by the *United Bible Society*. This Greek Bible is the product of the School of Higher Textual Criticism. This may also be the case with most young scholars who chose to study Greek. If so, they need to do as the writer did; purchase a copy of the Received Greek Text. There is a world of differences between these two Greek Bibles! And those differences came over into our new translations of the Scriptures.

The Scriptures Were Preserved through Two Streams

There are two streams through which the Scriptures were preserved. In the east, the Scriptures were preserved in the Greek Church. These manuscripts are referred to as the Byzantine manuscripts. These are the manuscripts from which the Received Text was edited. They were never questioned until 1881, when the Critical Text was published. That is, the Received Text was never questioned by anyone in the church. Thus the English translation, the Authorized Version, was revered as the Word of God.

Then there was also another stream through which the Scriptures were preserved. They were preserved in the Italic or the Old Latin Bible of the Waldensians. The Latin Bible of the Waldensians is distinguished from the Latin Bible of Jerome. The Waldenses' Bible is designated as the Italic. These godly people are said to date as far back as AD 120. They were originally from northern Italy. It was in northern Italy where all the Old Latin manuscripts were discovered. When they were relentlessly persecuted by the state church, they fled and made their abode in the rugged mountains of the Alps.

Dr. Frederick Nolan, a distinguished scholar in both Greek and Latin, in his research discovered that the Waldenses' Latin Bible was different than the Roman

Vulgate, and that it bore testimony of the apostolic primitive church and to "that celebrated text of the heavenly witnesses."[81] Though there are a few passages translated from the Latin in the Revelation in our Authorized Version, the reader should not be alarmed. This is because we do not have these few passages of the Scripture in the Greek manuscripts of the Revelation. But as stated earlier, the New Testament Scriptures were translated into Latin close to the same time when they were completed in the Greek. Our Lord did not at any time leave us without a witness.

Unitarians on the Revision Committee

As mentioned earlier, there were two Unitarians on the Revision Committee. These were Dr. G. Vance Smith of St. Savior's Gate Unitarian Chapel, York, and Dr. Joseph Henry Thayer, professor of Harvard Divinity School. Unitarianism is the modern revival of the ancient heresy of Arianism. It is a denial of the deity of our Lord Jesus Christ. These men adamantly deny the doctrine of the Trinity. Though Dr. Thayer was a professor in the States, he acted as a consultant to the Revision Committee as well as being an active member on the Revision Committee of the American Standard Bible produced in 1903. Any passage that affirmed the deity of our Lord was hostilely opposed.

For example, Dr. Vance Smith's comment on the passage 1 Timothy 3:16, "God manifested in flesh," he labored to successfully alter it to read, "Who was manifested in flesh." This is entirely satisfactory to Dr. Smith, who commented:

> The old reading has been pronounced untenable by the Revisers, as it has long been known to be by all careful students of the New Testament...

---

[81] Fredrick Nolan, *Integrity of the Greek Vulgate* (London: F.C. & J. Rivington, 1815), xvii-xviii.

> It is another example of the facility with which ancient copies introduced the word "God" into the manuscripts—a reading which was the natural result of growing tendency in early Christian times to look upon the humble Teacher as incarnate Word, and therefore as God "manifested in flesh."[82]

He also opposed and sanctioned the change in Matthew 28:19, the Trinitarian baptism in the name of the Father and of the Son and of the Holy Ghost by changing the preposition "in" to "into." Dr. Smith rejoiced over this change, as to him it obliterated the Trinitarian doctrine.[83] He favored the omission of the Trinitarian passage, 1 John 5:7, as well. Any passage that declared the deity of our Lord was opposed and sought to be removed or revised. There were at least six thousand revisions and omissions in the Critical Text. Thus the ancient heresy of Arianism has been revived. Its stamp is clearly seen in these modern translations of the Scriptures. The struggle in contending for the truth has not changed. We have the same enemy, the devil, with whom we must contend. He still and always will oppose our Lord Jesus Christ and those who identify with Him.

Why, then, are the Scriptures attacked? It is because through them we come to know our Lord Jesus Christ. To come to know Him is to come to love and serve Him. God stooping to partake of our nature and bear our sins in order to die in our place so that we might have life eternal is astounding! It is incomprehensible love! To make Jesus Christ anything less than God is to mar the love of God as well as to damn the souls of men. Unless we obtain

---

82 (Fuller, True or False 26-27) And Benjamin Wilkinson, *Our Authorized Bible Vindicated*, (Leaves Of Autumn Books, Inc., 1930), 40-41.
83 (Fuller, True or False 152)

In Defense of the Authenticity of 1 John 5:7

the righteousness of God, we will not have life eternal. In 2 Corinthians 5:21, we read, "For he hath made him to be sin for us, who knew no sin; that we might be made the righteousness of God in him." "Him" is none other than Jesus Christ, the eternal Word that became flesh. Nothing less than God's righteousness will suffice! It is God's righteousness that is imputed to us as our sins were imputed to Him who died in our stead. This is a marvel of marvels! Oh let us praise our adorable Lord Jesus Christ without end!

Why the Mentioning of Drs. Westcott and Hort?

One may wonder why the writer mentions Drs. Westcott and Hort, who were the critics of the latter part of the nineteenth century. Why were not the critics of the twenty–first century mentioned? Well, some were, such as Dr. Metzger. But what the reader should keep in mind is that as Columbus was the first to chart the way across the Atlantic the later others followed, so in like manner Drs. Westcott and Hort were the first to set forth the course for the textual critics in the School of Higher Textual Criticism upon which they now have embarked. The contemporary textual critics are still to this day following in the steps of these two men. Men are still referring to the oldest manuscripts. They still lump the heretical manuscripts in with the authentic manuscripts. And they are still referring to different branches of the church. Furthermore, they are still using Drs. Westcott and Hort's Greek Critical Text in formulating their own Critical Text.

Thus the revisions that are made by the contemporary textual critics are based upon the sophistries of these two men of the past. They, as Drs. Westcott and Hort, deny divine revelation and preservation of the Sacred Scriptures. They both hold to source or form criticism, as pointed out in the statement by Dr. Metzger. These are but a few similarities that are still retained by the School of Higher Textual Critics. Therefore, Drs. Westcott and Hort cannot be ignored, as they played the major role in producing the Critical Greek text. They are the mentors of the new breed of textual critics.

Constantine the Great

Historians are somewhat divided when it comes to Constantine the Great. He no doubt was a great general as well as an outstanding statesman. He came into power over part of the empire in AD 312and 313 he became co-regent with his brother–in–law, Licinius, issuing the edict of tolerance. The saints were still under horrendous persecution until that time. It was not until AD 323 that Constantine assumed full power over the entire Roman Empire. He is rightly called Constantine the Great. But the question remains, was he Christian? Was he orthodox if he was a Christian, or was he heretical? There are historians on both sides of the fence on this subject.

There are those who argue that Constantine was orthodox in his theology. At the same time, there are others who question his orthodoxy. To this day his orthodoxy is open to debate, for the acts of Constantine were not always in agreement with Christian profession. All of this leads the writer to question his Christianity. However, there may have been repentance before his death. A few days before his death, he was baptized and never again put on the purple. He was robed in white, waiting for his departure. But at the same time, he was baptized by an Arian priest, Eusebuis of Nicomedia.

As for the acts of Constantine the Great, these too lead us to question his orthodoxy. For example, he banished Athanasius on five different occasions. This would not speak

In Defense of the Authenticity of 1 John 5:7

in favor of his orthodoxy, in that Athanasius was banished because he would not compromise his position on the deity of our Lord. Then adding to this crime, he sought to fill Athanasius's office in Alexandra with an Arian priest. The priest was Arius, whom the emperor befriended. The people of Alexandra would not stand for it and ran him out of the city. This infuriated the emperor, but he was helpless outside of shedding blood to do anything about it. This leads us to believe the emperor was not orthodox in his theology.

Another shadow cast upon Constantine is that he set an Arian bishop over the Greek Church. He installed Eusebius of Nicomedia as bishop over the church in Constantinople. Later when Arius was condemned because of his heretical teachings, he appealed to Eusebius of Nicomedia, who came to his aid.[84] Eusebius was a great supporter of Arius, as he himself embraced the Arian heresy. He was also the same who baptized Constantine a few days before his death. Jerome wrote, "Constantine was baptized into Arianism."[85] But more so, Eusebius continued as bishop over the church after the emperor's death. This in itself is telling.

This may be because members of his family were strong Arians. His wife, mother, and son, who assumed the purple after Constantine, were great supporters of Arius. And when his son came into power, he did not demote Eusebius but rather oppressed the orthodox bishops. As for the Arian bishops, they were supported by the state. So there are shadows cast upon this great statesman, all of which leads us to assume that the Arian hold on the church was much stronger than previously mentioned. Yet by the grace of God, the Church of our Lord Jesus Christ prevailed!

---

84 Winston Walker, *A History of the Christian Church* (New York: Charles Scribner's Sons, 1959), 107.
85 (Schaff, History of the Christian Church, Vol. 3 36)

The Revisionist of 1881

It is only fair to mention that all the men on the Revision Committee of 1870--1881 were not bent to corrupting the Scriptures. Many of these men were not equipped to do the work that it turned out to be. They were not textual critics. When they engaged upon the work of revising of the Authorized Version of the Scriptures, they were not to refashion a New Greek Text. They were commissioned to make as few changes as possible to the Authorized Version. They definitely were not to refashion the Sacred Scriptures!

The reader must keep in mind that the English language is a living language; thus, over the years, words begin to take on new meanings. Words such as "wont," know, and "prevent," to go before, were to be updated so that the contemporary reader would understand what these words mean. It was these readings they were to amend. As it turned out, they created an entirely different Bible. There were over thirty-six thousand changes made in the entire Bible, and a little less than six thousand of these were made in the New Testament alone.

How was this accomplished? Dr. Hort made a recommendation. Dr. Scrivener opposed. Then there was one who broke the tie, and they went on. This was because many on the committee were not textual critics. Dr. Newth, one of the revisers on the committee, later wrote that the men on the committee did not have the all of the facts set before them. They were not aware of the character of the two ancient witnesses, the Vaticanus and the Sinaiticus, set before then as witnesses. They discovered their corruption only after the work was completed. As it was, able men and competent critics came forth denouncing these changes as well as exposing their corruptions. But the die was cast; it was too late to amend what was done. But it is never too late to educate the saints to return to the Holy Scriptures that were given and preserved by our Lord to all generations.

Dr. Scrivener is without question one of the most honest men on the Revision Committee. Yet he was dishonest in addressing the Comma. He wrote:

"Even the great Latin writers Hilary, Lucifer, Ambrose, Jerome, Augustine, all of the fourth century know nothing of it."[86]

At best this is an exaggeration. Other textual critics mentioned Augustine testifying in behalf of the Comma. And what shall we say of the great outrage that arose against Jerome when he omitted the Comma! Surely Jerome knew why the people were outraged with his Vulgate! Furthermore in the prologue of his Latin Vulgate, Codex Fuddensis, Jerome wrote concerning the Comma.[87] It is one thing to say that these Latin Fathers to his knowledge did not mention the Comma; but it is an outlandish prefabrication to imply that these men had no knowledge of it.

The Two Schools of Textual Criticism

The reader may not be familiar with the two different schools of textual criticism. The writer at one time thought a textual critic was simply a textual critic. But this is not so, as there are two different schools of textual criticism. On school of textual criticism is referred to as the School of Lower Textual Criticism. The critics had no doubt that they were handling the Sacred Oracles that were handed down and preserved to all generations. They saw their task to be no more than to edit the Byzantine manuscripts, as these were the ones always used by the Greek Church. These manuscripts for centuries were referred to as the Majority Text.

---

86 (Scrivener, Six Lectures on the Text of the New Testament 205)
87 (Metzger 648)

But presently, this is not the case, as a new Majority Text has been created by a branch of the School of Higher Textual Critics. These men merely collate all of the Greek manuscripts, heretical as well as orthodox, and compose a Bible that was never known to the church. Presently, there are two Majority Texts that are on the market, and no doubt more will come forth. This school is absurdity added to absurdity.

As the reader is aware by this time, all the words in the Greek manuscripts ran together without any spaces in between. The textual critic's task, among other things, was to properly divide these words from one another. They also were to correct things such as spelling and so forth. As one might see, this was a long and laborious task. At times, one letter might be left out of a word, which would slightly affect the reading of the Scriptures.

One example is a slight difference between the reading of the Stephen and Beza Edition of the Received Text on Acts 17:25. Stephen translates the text to read *"everywhere,"* while Beza translates the same text to read *"and all things."* The difference stems from one letter missing. Stephens in his Greek text read the passage "κατα παντα," while Beza read it as, "και τα παντα." If the reader will look closely at the two readings, he or she would discover the difference between the two readings is one letter. The iota is missing in Stephen's text. Instead of και τα, the iota was carelessly omitted, and he read it to read κατα. It was to such things as these that the School of Lower Textual Criticism gave themselves. As one can readily see, their labors were tedious and time consuming. They were not creating a new Bible but rather, they were editing it.

Then there is the new school of textual criticism, which is known as the School of Higher Textual Criticism. This school has no regard to divine revelation and inspiration

In Defense of the Authenticity of 1 John 5:7

of the Scriptures. Therefore, neither do they believe in the divine preservation of the Scriptures. This school of critics is still in search of the Scriptures. Even though they have produced a Critical Greek Text, as well as their Majority Text, they are still seeking to recover the Original Autograph. They confess that they have not recovered it as yet, but they have produced a Bible as close as they can to the Original Autograph. As one can readily see, the difference between these two schools of textual criticism is enormous. These men of the School of Higher Textual Criticism have no business handling the Holy Scriptures. And we have no business having any dealings with them or with any of the perversions of the Scriptures they have created!

The Oldest manuscripts

The oldest Greek manuscripts that we have in our possession are the Vaticanus and the Sinaiticus. What is tragic is how contemporary scholars idolize these manuscripts. Neither is there any disagreement between scholars in the dating of these manuscripts. They unanimously date them anywhere between Ad 325 to 350. Tregelles, a very competent textual critic, personally studied the manuscript Vaticanus. In conferring with Dr. Scrivener concerning this manuscript, said that he was sure that "it was written at the time of the council of Nice (AD 325)."[88]

This dating of the Codex B by Tregelles in itself is very significant. It leaves little or no doubt that this manuscript was one of the fifty manuscripts that survived of which Constantine the Great had commissioned Eusebuis to produce. This manuscript, as its sister, the Sinaiticus, were elaborate works written in capital letters on Vellum. Both of these manuscripts are dated about the same time. However,

---

88 (Scrivener, Six Lectures on the Text of the New Testament 28)

as it was pointed out earlier, these manuscripts are very corrupt, even to the point that they are beyond hope of being amended. The reason for their survival is quite apparent: the church never used them. This is quite evident, is it not, or they would have been worn out long ago through use!

As for the Sinaiticus manuscript, there were over 14,800 corrections by scribes over the years. It was hopelessly corrupt. And as for the Vaticanus manuscript, it is no better. It is said by some modern scholars that it looks more like a fifteenth–century manuscript, as later copyists had written over it. These manuscripts are so corrupt that they should never even be considered. The only reason modern scholars esteem them as they do is because of their antiquity. They are in search of the Word of God, and thus the oldest to them is the most reliable as it is closer to the Original Autograph.

The Old Latin Manuscripts

The Latin Bible that was used by Roman Christians was called the Vedus or the Old Latin. We are told that this is a different Latin than that which was used in Africa at the time.[89] This may be open to debase, however the writer does not wish to explore that avenue. The reader may pursue this endeavor if he wishes. However, we do know that the Church in Rome was under the control or better under the influence of the Greek Church.[90] This is apparent in that Ireneaus was sent by Polycarp to Rome to restore the Church in Rome that was plagued with over one hundred heresies at that time. It was not the African Church that sought to restore the Roman Church, but rather the Greek Church. This was because the Church in Rome was no doubt established by the Greek Church.

---

89 Drs. McIntosh and Twyman, *The Archko Volume* (New Canaan, CT: Keats Publishing Inc., 1998), 34

90 (Drs. McIntosh and Twyman 34)

In Defense of the Authenticity of 1 John 5:7

The writer of *The Archon Volume* wrote, "While in Constantinople I found one of these Volumes nicely cased, marked by the Emperor's name (Constantine the Great) and date upon it. To me it was a great curiosity. I got permission with a little bachsach, as they called money, to look through it. It was written on hieotike, which is the finest parchment, in large, bold, Latin characters, quite easy to read.....If the Revision Committee had examined it and published this work, they might have said they were giving the world something new; but so far as we examined it we saw nothing essentially different from our present Bible."[91]

What is interesting of this finding, is these two men, Drs. McIntosh and Twyman, in 1887, just six years after the Revised Version was published they had discovered this ancient Old Latin manuscript, dating it back to the time of Constantine the Great. This is the only complete Old Latin manuscript of which the writer is aware. The dating of this manuscript would have to be around AD 325–330. What is of further interest is that men on the Revision Committee had not explored the library in Constantinople while revising the Scripture. Instead they explored the library in Rome! This is indeed interesting.

This Old Latin manuscript is said to be essentially the same as our Authorized Version. This is the witness of two separate witnesses. We have the testimony of Drs. McIntosh and Twyman, as well as that of Dr. Frederick Nolan, who was earlier mentioned. They both testified that there is no essential difference in the Old Latin Scriptures and our Authorized Version of the Bible. The Johanneum Comma was in the Latin Scriptures in the Greek Church that predates the oldest manuscript we have in our possession. This Old Latin Manuscript was of Greek origin and thus the same

---

91 (Drs. McIntosh and Twyman 60-61)

as the Byzantine Text. And as earlier observed, all of the Old Latin that we have in our possession has the disputed passage of 1 John 5:7. So much for the oldest manuscripts and the verdict of contemporary scholars passed on the Trinitarian passage!

The Preservation of the Scriptures

When one passes and reflects upon the history of how the Sacred Scriptures were preserved, one is struck with awe. Many fail to take into account the Muslim holy wars that were conducted from the time of Mohammad. Christian communities were ravished and the Scriptures destroyed. The Byzantine Ottoman wars continued for over 150 years. They fought from AD 1299 to 1453. The Byzantine Empire finally fell in the year 1453 into the hands of Mehmed II, the Sultan of the Ottoman Empire. He was but nineteen years of age when he triumphantly entered Constantinople. He toppled that magnificent Empire that reigned for over a thousand years.

The Greek manuscripts for the most part were treasured in her libraries. The Greek Church was the guardian of the Greek manuscripts, even as the Jews were of the Old Testament Scriptures. Thus the fall of the empire was devastating in many ways. However, before the fall of the Byzantine Empire, she had been weakened by other wars in which she had been engaged. For example, in AD 1204, the empire fell into the hands of the Crusaders. This was in many respects exceedingly worse than falling into the hands of the Muslims.

The Latin Church of Rome was exceedingly bitter with the church in the East. There had been a long, ongoing feud between the two. Thus when the Crusaders finally conquered the Byzantine Empire, they raped, plundered, and destroyed. This unbridled savagery continued for a

In Defense of the Authenticity of 1 John 5:7

considerable length of time. They were exceedingly more destructive and brutal than the Muslims who later took the empire. The Crusaders had absolutely no regard for the works of art or the Sacred Scriptures. They destroyed whatever they could put their hands on.

But when Mehmed II conquered Constantinople, he only allowed his army three days to plunder, and then he quickly brought order to the city. He also preserved the Greek Church and her manuscripts. This may have been because his wife was a Christian. This too was of the providence of God, even as Esther was wife and queen to King Ahasuerus of Persia. But the Crusaders of Rome, on the other hand, had no regard for works of culture or for the Sacred Manuscripts. They were utterly barbaric and brutish conquerors.

Drs. McIntosh and Twyman mention the dreadful struggle that took place between the Greek Church and the Crusaders when the Crusaders entered into Constantinople. The Greek Church struggled desperately to preserve the sacred parchments from being destroyed.[92] The Crusaders had little or no regard for the Greek manuscripts. They wanted to Latinize the church in the east. But they failed to accomplish their end.

Thus in AD 1261, the Greeks were able to wage war and expel the Latin Church from its borders. However, she was soon thereafter engaged in wars from surrounding nations. These wars weakened her considerably. By 1453, the pressures being as they were, the Empire ultimately collapsed. But before the utter collapse of the Empire, many fled into Europe. They brought with them many of the Sacred Manuscripts. The fall of Constantinople in turn was

---

92 (Drs. McIntosh and Twyman 35)

a blessing to the West as light began to break in those dark regions under the control of Popes.

Historically men such as Diocletian, Arians, and the long line of heathen emperors, Crusaders, Muslims, and now so–called Textual Critics have sought to destroy the Word of God. But all of their efforts have miserably failed. It was by divine providence that the hands of the wicked were restrained from doing more damage than they did. This is only mentioned so that the reader might become profoundly conscious of God preserving the Sacred Scriptures even in the darkest of times.

This brings us to one of the major doctrines of Scripture that is ignored by the Critical Text Advocates. This is the doctrine of the divine preservation of the Scriptures. That is God preserves His Word to all generations. There are many biblical passages that attest to this truth. As for a few these are:

> Psalm 12:6–7: "The words of the LORD are pure words: as silver tried in a furnace of earth, purified seven times. Thou shalt keep them, O LORD, thou shalt preserve them from this generation forever."

Matthew 5:18: "For verily I say unto you, Till heaven and earth pass, one jot or one title shall in no wise pass from the law, till all be fulfilled."

Matthew 24:35: "Heaven and earth shall pass away, but my words shall not pass away."

John 10:35: "If he called them gods, unto whom the word of God came, and the Scripture cannot be broken." That is, the Scriptures cannot be destroyed.

Many more passages may be cited, but these mentioned are sufficient to prove the point. This doctrine the saints in the past embraced without question. It was never open to discussion because this truth was understood. God's Word, as God Himself, cannot be destroyed. But those men on the Revision Committee scoffed at this doctrine. Dean Burgan's reply to those scoffers is indeed fitting. He wrote:

> It is indeed credible that Almighty Wisdom which is observed to have made such abundant provisions for the safety of the humblest form of animal life, for the preservation of common seeds, often seeds of noxious plants—should yet have omitted to make provision for the life giving seed of His own Everlasting Word?[93]

Of this very subject, Peter by the Holy Ghost wrote: "Being born again, not of corruptible seed, but of incorruptible, by the word of God, which liveth and abideth for ever. For all flesh is as grass, and all glory of man as the flower of grass. The grass withereth, and the flower thereof falleth away: But the word of the Lord endured for ever. And this is the word which by the gospel is preached unto you" (1 Peter 1:23–25).

In light of the testimony of the Holy Oracles and the clear witness of history, how can anyone in good conscience deny God preserving His Word to all generations? And even though men through their maliciousness sought and still seek to destroy the Word of God, they are not equal to the task. Nevertheless, wicked men throughout the centuries have laboriously labored to corrupt the Scriptures. They have sought to utterly remove the Johanneum Comma from the Sacred Oracles. But to this day, they have miserably failed. Nor shall they ever succeed, because the Author and Preserver of the Holy Scriptures is greater than they. When

---

93 (Dean Burgon and Jay P. Green xiv)

shall mortal men discover that they are less than dust in the balances before Him with Whom they contend!

The Conspiracy

From the time of the Reformation, the Church of Rome sought to bring the Scriptures into question. The promulgation of the Scriptures shattered the papal kingdom. An entire book may be written on this subject. However, there are few things that should be considered when questioning the Authorized Version and the Comma in particular. One is that Count Tischendorf, prior to his discovery of Codex Sinaiticus, on several occasions had private audiences with the pope. Also, it is known that prior to his discovery of the Sinaiticus Manuscript; he had produced seven editions of the Greek New Testament, in which there were minor variations between them. They mostly had to do with punctuation. Furthermore, these editions of the New Testament did not exclude the Comma. It was retained in all seven of his editions of the New Testament.

But after several private audiences with the pope, as it so happened, he revisited St. Catherine, a monastery in Sinai. He had made several visits there before, but now when he revisited it in 1859, there was set before him the mutilated manuscript, the Sinaiticus. It is interesting that this just happened to be set before him when in 1844, he found part of the same body of manuscripts (The Septuagint) in a wastepaper basket and was about to light a fire.[94] It was from this discovery in 1859 that he produced his eighth edition of the Greek New Testament. This edition of the New Testament was a tremendous departure from his earlier editions. This was because he heavily leaned upon this corrupt manuscript, the Sinaiticus.

---

94 (Scrivener, Six Lectures on the Text of the New Testament 32-33)

In Defense of the Authenticity of 1 John 5:7

What is also of further interest is that while both Drs. Westcott and Hort were students studying Greek, they rejected the Textus Receptus.[95] When they were creating their Greek text, they chose to use the Karl Lockman's edition of the Greek New Testament and Count Tischendorf's eighth edition of the Greek New Testament.[96] Tischendorf's edition of the New Testament had been out no more than twelve years when the Revision Committee met! It was these two Greek Testaments that these two men heavily leaned upon in producing their Critical Greek Text.[97]

In turn, Drs. Westcott and Hort later gave small readings of their Critical Text to a few of the men on the Revision Committee as they revised the Scriptures. The New Testament that was revised was the product of their own Critical Greek Bible that they had earlier put together. This Bible of these two above–mentioned men had become the foundation from which all the new translations of the Bible are produced.[98]

If these men were honest in their search for the Scriptures, as they confess, then why did they not consider the library in Constantinople? Why was there such strong leaning upon the Vatican and the Vatican library? Is it not apparent that they were not interested in the Greek Text, which the church had faithfully embraced throughout the centuries! Is it not also apparent that from the onset they were determined to bring the Sacred Scriptures into doubt?

Of further interest is that later, unscrupulous men sat on the committee that put together the Critical Greek New Testament produced by the United Bible Society. This is the

---

95 (Brooke F. Westcott and Fenton J. A. Hort 16)
96 (Brooke F. Westcott and Fenton J. A. Hort 16)
97 (Brooke F. Westcott and Fenton J. A. Hort 16)
98 (Brooke F. Westcott and Fenton J. A. Hort 18) and (Scrivener, Six Lectures on the Text of the New Testament 112-113)

popular Greek Critical Text used in seminaries. Dr. Bruce Metzger was but one of the five men who labored on this Critical Edition of the New Greek Bible. Enough had earlier been said of him. But there was another on that committee who must not be overlooked: the Jesuit priest Dr. Carlos M. Martini. What is interesting is that Dr. Carlos M. Martini was later promoted to cardinal by the Church of Rome.

Why would Rome want to corrupt the Scriptures? It is because they challenge her authority. Men since Wycliffe, Huss, and Luther have shaken the papal kingdom by taking their stand upon the Holy Word of God. If the papal kingdom is to fully recover from the blow she received from the reformers, then the Scriptures must be destroyed or at least be brought into question. And if the Holy Scriptures are brought into doubt, then we, unlike those before us, are left with no place to stand!

> A mighty fortress is our God,
> A bulwark never failing;
> Our helper He amid the flood
> Of mortal ills prevailing.
> For still our ancient foe
> Doth seek to work us woe—
> His craft and pow'r are great,
> And armed with cruel hate,
> On earth is not his equal.
>
> Did we in our own strength confide
> Our striving would be losing,
> Were not the right Man on our side,
> The Man of God's own choosing.
> Dost ask who that may be?
> Christ Jesus, it is He—
> Lord Sabaoth His name,

From age to age the same—
And He must win the battle.

And tho this world, with devils filled,
    Should threaten to undo us,
We will not fear, for God hath willed
    His truth to triumph thru us.
    The prince of darkness grim—
      We tremble not for him;
      His rage we can endure,
      For lo! his doom is sure—
    One little word shall fell him .

That word above all earthly pow'rs—
    No thanks to them abideth;
The Spirit and the gifts are ours
    Thru Him who with us sideth.
    Let goods and kindred go,
      This mortal life also;
      The body they may kill:
    God's truth abideth still—
    His kingdom is forever.

–Martin Luther

Bibliography

Anderson, Bernard W. Understanding the Old Testament. London: Prentice-Hall International, 1966.

Burgon, Dean, and Jay P. Green. An introduction to Textual Criticism. Ed. Jay P. Green. Lafayette, IN: Sovereign Grace Trust Fund, 1990. Vol. 1.

Burton, John. Favorite Hymns of the Faith. Wheaton, IL: Tabernacle Publishing, 1974.

Cyprian. The Ante-Nicene Fathers. Trans. Ernest Wallis. New York: Charles Scribner's Sons, 1911. Vol. 5.

Dabney, Robert L. Discussions. Carlisle, PA: Banner of Truth, 1982. Vol. 1.

Edmunds, LiDie H. Favorite Hymns of the Faith. Wheaton, IL: Tabernacle Publishing, 1974.

Erasmus. Erasmus of Christendom. Ed. Roland H Bainton. New York: Charles Scribner's Sons, 1969.

Fuller, David Otis. True or False. 2nd ed. Grand Rapids: Grand Rapids International Publications, 1983.

—. Which Bible. Grand Rapids: Grand Rapids International Publications, 1972.

George Travis Letters to Edward Gibbon, Esq, Forgotten Books, 2015

Graves, J. R. Introductory Essay. A Concise History of Baptists by G. H. Orchard. Texarkana: Bogard, 1987.

Hills, Edwards F. The King James Defended. Junction City, OR: Eye Opener Publishers, 1973.

Lindsey Sr., Homer. Sermon at First Baptist Church of Jacksonville, Florida. n.d.

Mansfield, Stephen. Never Give In. New York: Hyperion, 2003.

McIntosh and Twyman. The Archko Volume. New Canaan, CT: Keats Publishing, 1998.

Metzger, Bruce M. A Commentary on the Greek New Testament. New York: American Bible Society, 1993. Vol. 2.

Nazianzus, Gregory of. The Post Nicene and Post Nicene Fathers. Grand Rapids: Erdmann Publishing, 1978.

Nestle-Aland. Greek New Testament. New York: American Bible Society, 1927. Vol. 13.

Nolan, Fredrick. Integrity of the Greek Vulgate. London: F.C. & J. Rivington, 1815. 136

- C. H. Pappas, ThM

Reader's Digest Association. The Bible Through the Ages. Pleasantville, NY: Reader's Digest, 1996.

Schaff, Philip. History of the Christian Church. Grand Rapids: WM. B. Eerdmans Publishing, 1985. Vol. 1.

—. History of the Christian Church. Grand Rapids: WM. B. Eerdmans Publishing, 1985. Vol. 2.

—. History of the Christian Church. Grand Rapids: WM. B. Eerdmans Publishing, 1985. Vol. 3.

Scrivener, Frederick H. A. A Plain Introduction to the New Testament Textual Criticism. 4th ed. New York: George Bell and Sons, 1894. Vol. 2.

—. Six Lectures on the Text of the New Testament. London: George Bell and Sons, 1875.

—. The Authorized Version of the English Bible. Edinburgh: Cambridge University Press, n.d.

Van Baalen, Jan Karel. The Chaos of the Cults. Grand Rapids: WM. B. Eerdmans Publishing, 1958.

Vincent, Marvin R. Word Studies in the New Testament. Wilmington, DE: Associated Publishers, 1972.

Wainwright, Arthur W. A Guide to the New Testament. London: Epworth, 1965.

Walker, Winston. A History of the Christian Church. New York: Charles Scribner's Sons, 1959.

Warfield, Benjamin B. Collections of Opinions and Reviews. New York: Oxford, 1932. Vol. 2.

Westcott, Brooke F, and Fenton J. A. Hort. Introduction to the New Testament in the Original Greek. Peabody, MA: Hendrickson Publishers, 1998. Vol. 3.

Wilkinson, Benjamin G. Our Authorized Bible. Payson, AZ: Leaves-Of-Autumn Books, 1930.

Wright, G Ernest, and Reginald H Fuller. The Acts of God. Garden City, NY: Double Day, 1957. 137

Made in the USA
Middletown, DE
23 May 2018